D0376448

THE YOGURT
COOKBOOK

Kay Shaw Nelson

THE YOGURT COOKBOOK

Illustrations by
SIBYL WEIL

DOVER PUBLICATIONS, INC., NEW YORK

Published in Canada by General Publishing Company, Ltd., 30 Lesmill Road, Don Mills, Toronto,
Ontario.

This Dover edition, first published in 1976, is an
unabridged and unaltered republication of the
work originally published in 1972 by Robert B.
Luce, Inc., under the title *Yogurt Cookery: Good
and Gourmet*.

International Standard Book Number: 0-486-23416-9
Library of Congress Catalog Card Number: 76-11508

Manufactured in the United States of America
Dover Publications, Inc.
180 Varick Street
New York, N. Y. 10014

To my mother

Dolina Shaw

CONVERSION TABLES FOR FOREIGN EQUIVALENTS

DRY INGREDIENTS

Ounces	Grams	Grams	Ounces	Pounds	Kilograms	Kilograms	Pounds
1 =	28.35	1 =	0.035	1 =	0.454	1 =	2.205
2	56.70	2	0.07	2	0.91	2	4.41
3	85.05	3	0.11	3	1.36	3	6.61
4	113.40	4	0.14	4	1.81	4	8.82
5	141.75	5	0.18	5	2.27	5	11.02
6	170.10	6	0.21	6	2.72	6	13.23
7	198.45	7	0.25	7	3.18	7	15.43
8	226.80	8	0.28	8	3.63	8	17.64
9	255.15	9	0.32	9	4.08	9	19.84
10	283.50	10	0.35	10	4.54	10	22.05
11	311.85	11	0.39	11	4.99	11	24.26
12	340.20	12	0.42	12	5.44	12	26.46
13	368.55	13	0.46	13	5.90	13	28.67
14	396.90	14	0.49	14	6.35	14	30.87
15	425.25	15	0.53	15	6.81	15	33.08
16	453.60	16	0.57				

LIQUID INGREDIENTS

Liquid Ounces	Milliliters	Milliliters	Liquid Ounces	Quarts	Liters	Liters	Quarts
1 =	29.573	1 =	0.034	1 =	0.946	1 =	1.057
2	59.15	2	0.07	2	1.89	2	2.11
3	88.72	3	0.10	3	2.84	3	3.17
4	118.30	4	0.14	4	3.79	4	4.23
5	147.87	5	0.17	5	4.73	5	5.28
6	177.44	6	0.20	6	5.68	6	6.34
7	207.02	7	0.24	7	6.62	7	7.40
8	236.59	8	0.27	8	7.57	8	8.45
9	266.16	9	0.30	9	8.52	9	9.51
10	295.73	10	0.33	10	9.47	10	10.57

Gallons (American)	Liters	Liters	Gallons (American)
1 =	3.785	1 =	0.264
2	7.57	2	0.53
3	11.36	3	0.79
4	15.14	4	1.06
5	18.93	5	1.32
6	22.71	6	1.59
7	26.50	7	1.85
8	30.28	8	2.11
9	34.07	9	2.38
10	37.86	10	2.74

Contents

Introduction

Yogurt has undergone a remarkable renaissance and made gastronomic history in recent years. The milk of eternal life, as it was once called, is acclaimed by millions of devotees as a fascinating asset in creative cookery. The tangy, semisolid cultured milk is highly esteemed as a delicacy that is marvelously versatile and adaptable. In itself an enjoyable and nutritious treat, yogurt also imparts flavor and richness to all elements of the culinary repertoire. Little wonder that yogurt has become so popular!

Yogurt is now widely available in many forms and is rapidly becoming a staple item in our diet. The cultured milk is one of our fastest growing convenience foods and is generally recognized as a source of exceptional nourishment. The reasons are obvious. It is low in fat and calories, high in nutritional value, very easily digested, and effective in maintaining a healthy intestinal system. Yogurt has often been called a perfect food.

Although the culinary and nutritional attributes of this inviting dairy product are a fairly recent discovery in America, they were known thousands of years ago in the ancient world. Even before the domestication of animals and the beginnings of agriculture, early man relied on milk from his goats, sheep, camels, buffaloes, asses or yaks as the mainstay of his diet. Soured or fermented milk, rather than fresh, was soon recognized to be far more valuable as it would last much longer and it also had an appealing flavor. Yogurt was an accidental discovery. Desert nomads, travelling over the vast expanses of southwestern Asia, carried their milk supplies in bags made of sheep's stomachs slung over the backs of their animals. Because of the joggling and hot sun the milk not only fermented but changed into a semisolid or concentrated consistency. Unknown to the nomads, the transformation had been caused by bacteria from the sheep's stomach. These would be identified centuries later as specific kinds of *lactobacilli* (milk bacteria) which differentiates yogurt from clabber or fermented milk.

Once the tribesmen had acquired their first batches of yogurt they were able to make more of it by inoculating fresh milk with a small amount of the yogurt already prepared. As they settled in villages and towns in the Near and Middle East, Central Asia and Southeastern Europe, these ancient peoples undertook the preparation of yogurt as a necessary daily household chore. Housewives boiled and inoculated the milk, which was poured into small earthenware bowls and kept warm with animal skins or coarsely woven blankets during the incubation period. Yogurt is still traditionally made in the homes of these countries by the same method.

There are many early references to yogurt in the records of ancient civilizations. It is one of man's oldest prepared foods. Several mentions of yogurt appear in the Bible, particularly as a healthy food. It was most beloved in the Biblical lands. Canaan, or the promised land, was, according to the Scripture, a paradise "flowing with milk and honey." Many religious students believe that the milk was *laban* or *leben,* the name still used in the Near East for yogurt.

In the book of Genesis we can read that Abraham offered curds to the three strangers who came to tell him of the birth of his son, Isaac. The patriarch has even been credited with introducing yogurt to the world. For according to an old eastern legend, the progenitor, who died at the age of 175 years, learned the secret for making yogurt when an angel whispered the magical formula to him. A long and cherished belief in the Biblical lands was that yogurt was responsible for Abraham's longevity and fecundity.

As early as the first century A.D., the Roman naturalist-historian, Pliny, described yogurt as "a good instrument of pleasure" and reportedly declared that man could live without bread but not without sour milk. Millions of others obviously considered yogurt essential for daily living and for many centuries the peoples of the Near and Middle East, parts of Russia and the Balkans have deemed it a most important staple in their diet and the preferred form of milk. Yogurt has been and still is the food of both rich and poor, relished in great quantity and variety.

The first known appearance of yogurt in Western Europe did not occur until the early 1500's and then only through a bizarre circumstance. History tells us that King Francois I of France was seriously ill with an intestinal ailment which could not be cured even by the greatest medical experts of the time. Fast losing his zest for life, the king was interested to hear from his ambassador to the Ottoman court in Constantinople that there was a Turkish doctor or healer who had effected remarkable cures in similar cases. The secret, he was told, was a fermented milk which seemed to keep people very healthy.

At the request of the monarch, the doctor was summoned to Paris and arrived at the royal court on foot and accompanied by a herd of goats and sheep. His treatment of the king was to prescribe several bowls of yogurt each day. Much to the surprise of everyone, the royal patient recovered, regained his capacity for the pleasures of life, and asked the doctor for the secret of the milk. The request was to no avail as the eastern visitor refused to divulge any information about the yogurt. Instead, he returned to Constantinople with his herd. So impressed were the French with the miraculous food that they named it *le lait de la vie éternelle,* the milk of eternal life.

That yogurt was responsible for the cure of the French king must not have been any surprise in Turkey, the Balkans or other lands where it was a staple food. For over the centuries more and more medicinal powers were attributed to the cultured milk. It truly was the household cure-all relied on by millions of believers. Each housewife or healer had a particular formula for treating an illness with yogurt. Some never have been recorded and others have been lost in history. The Turks supposedly believed that yogurt mixed with flower buds and spread on the forehead would cure insomnia. Persian ladies treated their skin with yogurt facials. Combined with garlic, it became a remedy for stomach aches. Yogurt was taken as a cure for ulcers, as an antidote for food poisoning and excessive drinking, to relieve sunburn, as a beauty aide, and for an untold number of other reasons.

Most importantly, however, yogurt was believed to have the quasi-miraculous power of enhancing virility and prolonging life. A survey or report that came out in the late 1800's and was circulated fairly widely revealed that Bulgaria had the greatest number of aged people in proportion to its population, some of whom reportedly bore or sired children at a quite advanced age. It was also stated that the Bulgarians were the world's greatest consumers of yogurt.

These reports were of particular interest in the early 1900's to a

Russian-born French bacteriologist, Ilya Metchnikoff. A co-winner of the Nobel Prize in 1908, Metchnikoff was engaged in trying to find the reasons for premature aging or senility in humans. His research and findings at the Pasteur Institute in Paris had given him reason to suspect that a major cause was due to a repository of putrefying bacteria in the large intestine. This, he believed, resulted in poisoning the body and shortening life.

Anxious to learn why the hard-working Bulgarians lived so long, Metchnikoff travelled to that small Balkan country to observe the people and their daily diet. He saw for himself that many laborers in the fields were indeed healthy and agile, even though they had passed their 80th, 90th or even 100th birthdays. Metchnikoff also noted that throughout the day they ate considerable quantities of yogurt either by itself or mixed with such foods as chopped raw vegetables, garlic or nuts. The professor became convinced that the prevalence of yogurt in the diet was very significant. In his book, *The Prolongation of Life,* Metchnikoff asserted that "the good health and long life of the Bulgarians was due to the custardy fermented milk that they consumed in great quantity . . ."

So convinced was the professor that yogurt contained bacilli which could kill unfriendly bacteria in the intestines that through his experiments at the Pasteur Institute he finally succeeded in pinpointing and isolating the two types of friendly bacteria in yogurt. One, *lactobacillus bulgaricus,* named in honor of the Bulgarian octogenarians, caused an acid action in milk and was responsible for its coagulation. Another, *streptococcus thermophilus,* fermented the milk sugar into lactic acid and gave yogurt its flavor and aroma. Both manufactured large amounts of B vitamins which killed the putrefying bacteria and assisted in maintaining a healthy intestinal system.

After these milk bacteria were isolated, purified and then used in the preparation of a pure culture, it became possible to produce yogurt on a large scale. Metchnikoff, who championed the cause of yogurt until his death, is very often credited with introducing or reintroducing it to the West. At least he did stimulate interest in yogurt and because of his work others became devotees of this so-called miracle milk. One of them was a Spaniard, Isaac Carasso, who began making and selling yogurt in his native Barcelona. He soon moved his small business to Paris where he started selling it commercially during

World War I. In 1929, he opened a yogurt plant and named his product Danone for his son Daniel. About the mid-1950's the enterprise began to expand considerably and shortly thereafter the Danone company opened the world's largest yogurt factory, catering to the tastes of not only the French but other Europeans who have developed an absolute mania for this food, both plain and flavored. Yogurt today appears on the tables of the most elegant Parisian restaurants.

Yogurt was reportedly first brought to the United States about 1784 by some Turkish immigrants who included the dried culture among their prized possessions. They prepared the food as they had in their homeland—by adding a starter to fresh milk and keeping small bowls warm with shawls or blankets during the period of incubation. By the turn of the century, a greater number of ethnic groups had emigrated to America from the Balkans and Middle Eastern countries, and they prepared and ate their beloved native food in greater quantity. But yogurt first gained popularity in the United States when vaudevillians used it as a butt of their jokes to poke fun at the strange name and its cure-all "powers." Most probably the comedians who ridiculed it never even tasted the cultured milk.

After the outbreak of World War II, Isaac Carasso left France for the United States and soon thereafter opened a yogurt plant in New York City catering primarily to ethnic groups in the area. Changing the name to Dannon, he and a partner, Joseph Metzger, launched a long and extensive campaign to familiarize the American public with yogurt. By the mid-1960s they had achieved considerable success and yogurt became known in all parts of the country. Other companies joined in the competition and dairies also added yogurt to their roster of products.

It is interesting to note, however, that these enterprising businessmen introduced many changes in the production of yogurt so the kind that has become popular in our country is quite different from the yogurt of the Balkans and Middle East. There it is still made as it was centuries ago, primarily in the homes or in small factories, and is very rich and creamy. Because it is made with whole milk, generally from sheep and/or goats, the butterfat content is quite high and the flavor is definitely tart or piquant. It is called *yoğurt* in Turkey, *kisselo mleko* in Bulgaria, *mazun* in Armenia, *leben* or *laban* in the Near East, *dahī* in India and *yaourti* in Greece.

It was decided by the early manufacturers of American yogurt that it should be given a new look. Therefore, the first step was to prepare it with partially skimmed milk, which did not reduce any of the nutritive value but did lower the number of calories. Today most commercial yogurt is made with partially skimmed pasteurized milk (about 1.7% milk fat), enriched with non-fat milk solids. One cup of plain yogurt has from 120 to 125 calories.

Another step in the alteration of the product was to remove the tart taste of plain yogurt by sweetening it. In the 1950's the manufacturers started adding fruit preserves and fruit flavorings to the plain variety. Some kinds merely had fruit on the bottom of the carton; others combined the yogurt with a sugar base and, after factory-stirring, the fruit was distributed throughout the yogurt. Later, yogurts flavored with vanilla, coffee and chocolate appeared. Today there are about 26 choices, with strawberry the most popular. Although these products do have more calories than plain yogurt, they are eaten primarily as snacks or desserts and trail in calorie-count such competitive foods as cakes, pies and ice creams.

To make yogurt commercially the fresh milk is first pasteurized at from 170°F. to 190°F. It is then homogenized and cooled at temperatures ranging from 100°F. to 115°F. After being inoculated with culture, the mixture is poured into containers and incubated at temperatures from 105°F. to 110°F. for from 2¾ to 3 hours and until an acidity of .75% is achieved. The chilling and storage takes place at from 40°F. to 42°F.

Yogurt can also be prepared easily and inexpensively in the home either with or without special equipment. The simplest way is to inoculate heated and cooled milk with a small amount of a prepared batch of yogurt or a powdered culture and then to keep it warm during the incubation period. This method does not always work, however, as without special utensils, particularly a thermometer, it is difficult to maintain a correct temperature continuously during the period of incubation so the bacteria will thrive and thicken the milk to a semisolid consistency. The bacteria will not grow below 90°F. and are killed at temperatures above 120°F.

Yogurt can be prepared more accurately in the home with an electric yogurt maker, called also an electromatic thermo-cult incubator. There are three or more kinds of varying sizes which are sold generally in health or specialty food stores or may be ordered by mail from the International Yogurt Company.*

Any kind of milk can be used to prepare yogurt in the home. It may be fresh whole or skimmed, canned or powdered. Some persons prefer combinations of half skim and half homogenized, powdered and skim milks, or powdered and evaporated milks with water. As previously stated, the culture, or starter, may be a small amount of previously prepared commercial or homemade yogurt or a powdered culture. For each new batch of yogurt some of that already prepared is set aside. Powdered culture is sold in packages in health and specialty food stores, or it may be ordered by mail from the International Yogurt Company. It is an improved dry original Bulgarian yogurt culture which was developed and produced by the Rosell Bacteriological Dairy Institute in Montreal, Canada.

The majority of the yogurt that is purchased commercially is eaten directly out of the container as a quick snack or is served by itself, as an accompaniment for meals or as a dessert. Flavored yogurts are by far the most popular and new yogurt products are being developed. One company even sells frozen yogurt on a stick.

Yogurt, of course, is delicious as it is, but it may be sprinkled with sugar, spices, herbs, chopped nuts, raisins or honey, or flavored with jam, jelly or fruits, according to individual preference.

But the possibilities of cooking with yogurt are infinite. It is a good substitute for sour cream and, in some cases, milk and buttermilk. The cultured milk combines readily with both robust foods and delicacies. It is an excellent marinade. Yogurt marries well with eggs, cheese, meats, seafood, poultry and grains. It can be used in making dishes of universal appeal, ranging from appetizers and soups to desserts and beverages.

The resulting culinary creations amply demonstrate the rich inventiveness and deliciousness that yogurt adds to our gastronomic repertoire. The recipes include as many as possible of the natural foods and are designed to contribute to the improvement of a better and well balanced diet. They cover the whole range of good and gourmet cookery.

* See page 19.

Basic Data and Recipes

1. *Bacteria:* yogurt is made with a culture containing beneficial bacteria which are allowed to multiply freely in temperature-controlled milk until it achieves the proper semisolid consistency and tart flavor. The bacteria in yogurt manufacture large amounts of B vitamins which are excellent for maintaining a healthy intestinal system.

2. *Calcium:* yogurt is an excellent source of calcium. One cup of plain yogurt, made from partially skimmed milk, has 294 milligrams of calcium. One cup of plain yogurt, made from whole milk, has 272 milligrams of calcium.

3. *Calories:* yogurt is low in calories and consequently is often recommended for dieters and weight watchers. One cup of plain yogurt, made from partially skimmed milk, has 125 calories. One cup of plain yogurt, made from whole milk, has 150 calories. Flavored yogurts have more calories, the amount varying according to the brand and kind.

4. *Carbohydrate:* one cup of plain yogurt, made from partially skimmed milk, contains 13 grams carbohydrate. One cup of plain yogurt, made from whole milk, contains 12 grams carbohydrate.

5. *Clabber:* thick sour, curdled or fermented milk. Clabber differs from yogurt in that it sours and thickens naturally. It is sometimes called bonnyclabber.

6. *Contents:* one cup of plain yogurt, made from partially skimmed milk, contains 89% water, 125 calories, 8 grams protein, 4 grams fat, 13 grams carbohydrate, 294 milligrams calcium, .1 milligram

iron, 170 international units vitamin A, .10 milligram thiamin, .44 milligram riboflavin, .2 milligram niacin and 2 milligrams ascorbic acid.

7. *Cooking*: yogurt is a versatile ingredient in cookery. It should be warmed gently over low heat and cooked over even, moderate heat for a short time so it will not separate. Separating can be prevented by first stabilizing the yogurt. To do this, cornstarch or flour is mixed with water and added to the yogurt before cooking. If, however, the yogurt separates the flavor is not affected but the dish is not as attractive. When adding yogurt to other ingredients it is generally best to fold or stir it in gently.

8. *Culture*: a colony of bacteria which is introduced into a nutrient substance. In order to make yogurt it is necessary to add a culture to the fresh milk. This may be a small amount of previously prepared yogurt or a powdered culture that is sold in packages in health and specialty food stores throughout the United States. The culture is sometimes called a "starter."

9. *Cultured milk*: made by adding bacterial culture to milk. Buttermilk, sour cream and yogurt are cultured products.

10. *Curd*: the coagulated part of milk that forms when the milk sours.

11. *Dahi*: the Indian and Pakistani name for yogurt.

12. *Digestion*: yogurt is very easily digested and assists the digestive system to assimilate other foods more effectively. Yogurt is converted into an absorbable form in only 30 to 40 minutes as compared to 3 to 4 hours for milk.

13. *Fat content*: yogurt has a low fat content and because of this it is often regarded as a good diet food. One cup of plain yogurt, made from partially skimmed milk, has 4 grams of fat. One cup of plain yogurt, made from whole milk, has 8 grams of fat.

14. *Fermentation*: the process which occurs in yogurt after the fresh milk has been inoculated with a culture. The chemical reactions caused by the fermentation change the milk to yogurt.

15. *Freezing*: it is not recommended that yogurt be frozen as the freezing and thawing adversely affect the smooth body and texture.

16. *Incubation*: the period that the newly inoculated milk is kept warm so the bacteria will cause the milk to ferment, thicken and become yogurt.

17. *International Yogurt Company:* 628 North Doheny Drive, Los Angeles, Calif. 90069. Yogurt cultures, electromatic thermo-cult incubators and other yogurt products can be ordered by mail from this company which promotes the home production of yogurt.

18. *Iron*: yogurt contains a small amount of iron. There is .1 milligram of iron in 1 cup of plain yogurt made from partially skimmed or whole milk.

19. *Laban* or *leben*: the name for yogurt in such Near Eastern countries as Iraq, Lebanon and Syria.

20. *Lactic acid*: a clear, syrupy liquid formed by the fermentation of lactose when milk sours. It is present in all sour or fermented milks. Yogurt contains more than three times the amount of lactic acid present in other fermented foods. Lactic acid assists the digestion of foods and is sometimes considered as an aid in weight reduction.

21. *Lactobacillus bulgaricus*: one of the two types of beneficial bacteria found in yogurt and used in the preparation of it. They cause an acid action in the milk and are responsible for its coagulation. The bacteria were isolated and named by Professor Metchnikoff.

22. *Lactose*: a white crystalline disaccharide made from whey and found in milk. It is also called "milk sugar" and "sugar of milk." This is important to the preparation of yogurt as the bacteria thrive on the warm lactose and change a certain amount of it into lactic acid. Lactose supplies energy and favors intestinal hygiene. (See 20 above)

23. *Mast*: the Iranian or Persian name for yogurt.

24. *Metchnikoff, Ilya*: also known as Elie Mechnikov. 1845 to 1916. The Russian-born French bacteriologist and Nobel Prize winner (1908) who is credited with "rediscovering" yogurt. A member of the Pasteur Institute in Paris, he identified, isolated and named the beneficial bacteria in yogurt and championed its therapeutic values. His discoveries made it possible to produce yogurt on a large scale.

25. *Minerals*: one cup of yogurt, made of partially skimmed milk, contains .1 milligram of iron, 294 milligrams of calcium, 270 milligrams of phosphorous, 50 milligrams of potassium and 19 milligrams of sodium.

26. *Protein*: yogurt is a very good source of protein. One cup of plain yogurt, made from partially skimmed milk, contains 8 grams of protein. One cup of plain yogurt, made from whole milk, contains 7 grams of protein.

27. *Refrigeration*: yogurt that is prepared in the home should be refrigerated after preparation to stop any further growth of bacteria. Commercial yogurt should be refrigerated as soon as possible and consumed within three or four days to give maximum flavor pleasure. If stored for longer periods, the acidity will continue to increase and the result will be a sharper flavored product.

28. *Streptococcus thermophilus:* one of the most desirable lactic bacteria and one of the two types of beneficial bacteria in yogurt. They quickly ferment milk sugar into lactic acid; inhibit growth of putrefactive bacteria; and are responsible for the flavor and aroma of yogurt.

29. *Temperature*: in the preparation of yogurt it is necessary to maintain an even and fairly high temperature so the bacteria will thrive in the milk. This is very important as bacteria will grow rapidly only in temperatures between 90°F. and 120°F. They are killed by higher temperatures and grow slowly or not at all in those below 90°F.

30. *Thermometer*: when preparing yogurt in the home a great aid is a thermometer which will help to maintain an even and proper temperature during the period of incubation. It must have degrees ranging between 90°F. to 120°F.

31. *Vitamins*: one cup of plain yogurt, made from partially skimmed milk, contains 170 international units of vitamin A, .10 milligram of vitamin B/thiamin, .44 milligram of vitamin B/riboflavin, .2 milligram of vitamin B/niacin, and 2 milligrams of vitamin C/ ascorbic acid.

32. *Whey*: the watery part of milk which separates from the curds after coagulation.

Basic Yogurt Recipes

Yogurt can be made easily, inexpensively and successfully in the home, with or without special equipment. It is done simply by inoculating milk with a culture or starter, and then keeping the mixture at a correct and continuous temperature during the period of incubation, a few hours. There is a problem, however, about attaining and keeping the right temperature, so generally it is preferable to experiment with a small batch at first. American home cooks have devised several techniques for the preparation of yogurt. Included here are a few good tips and methods to assist anyone who wishes to make this cultured milk.

The Ingredients

To make yogurt it is necessary to have only two ingredients, the milk and the culture. The milk should be fresh. It may be pasteurized, homogenized, skimmed, canned or milk reconstituted from dry powdered milk, or combinations of them. Some persons use half skimmed and half homogenized, powdered and skimmed milks, or powdered and evaporated milks. (When using dry powdered milk, it is, of course, necessary to reconstitute it with water.)

The culture, sometimes called a starter, may be a small amount of previously prepared commercial or homemade yogurt or a yogurt culture in powdered form. If yogurt is used it should be fresh as old yogurt will impart a sour taste to the new batch. Powdered yogurt culture may be purchased in health and specialty food stores or ordered from the International Yogurt Company. The culture should be well mixed with the milk so that it is broken up and distributed evenly throughout the liquid.

The Equipment

Yogurt can be made simply with ordinary kitchen utensils or special equipment especially designed and manufactured for the preparation of yogurt in the home.

Ordinary utensils include a measuring cup, a heavy saucepan (for heating the milk), a mixing spoon, and containers to hold the yogurt. The latter should be preferably earthenware, porcelain, pyrex or another type of glass. They can be small bowls, custard cups, jars or glasses.

It is also desirable to have a thermometer with degrees ranging from 90°F. to 120°F. so that the temperature of the milk can be tested and maintained at the proper level.

An item of special equipment is an electromatic incubator. There are three or more kinds. One is sold with small glass containers. Another comes complete with a single jar. A larger kind is designed to hold any type of containers. These may be purchased at health and specialty food stores or ordered by mail from the International Yogurt Company. Each is equipped with automatic heat control.

Making Yogurt

Method I

Put 1 quart of milk (fresh skimmed or homogenized, or any other kind) in a heavy saucepan and bring just to a boil, until bubbles form around the edge of the pan. Cool to lukewarm. Test by sprinkling on the wrist. It should feel warm but not hot. Or test with a thermometer which should read 110°F. to 115°F. Add the culture, 2 to 4 tablespoons* of prepared commercial or homemade yogurt at room temperature, or powdered yogurt culture, and mix well so that it is thoroughly combined with the milk. Pour into a prewarmed bowl or 4 glasses, cups or jars. Cover and put into a pot or kettle. Pour lukewarm water into the pot, until it reaches

---

* 2 tablespoons if the starter is fairly fresh. If more than four days old, add 3 or 4 tablespoons.

almost to the tops of the containers. Cover and wrap a thick towel or heavy cloth around the top. Set in a warm place, such as over the pilot light of a gas stove, and keep at a luke-warm temperature, 110°F. to 115°F. Do not disturb or stir. (If the warm place is not adequate, it may be necessary to replace the water which has cooled with lukewarm water.) After 3 hours check to see if the yogurt has begun to thicken. If not, leave longer until it has achieved a semisolid con-sistency. When ready, remove and chill. Makes 1 quart or 4 servings.

Method II*

Plug in an electromatic incubator. Heat 1 quart of milk in a heavy saucepan. Bring just to a boil. Then cool to luke-warm. Pour in the contents of 1 package of yogurt culture and mix well. Pour into prewarmed glasses, cups or jars and place in the plugged-in electromatic incubator. Cover and leave undisturbed for 2 hours. Remove the cover and see if the yogurt has started to thicken. If so, remove and put in the refrigerator to chill. If not, cover again and continue the incubation until it has started to thicken, checking every half hour. Do not over incubate or it will have too much acidity.

To make the second batch of yogurt from the above Method II, save 2 tablespoons of the first batch for each quart of milk. Add it to the boiled and cooled milk instead of the powdered culture. Succeeding batches for one month can be made in the same way. It is recommended that after this period a new powdered yogurt culture be purchased to make an entirely new batch.

Method III

Sweetened or flavored yogurt can also be made in an electromatic incubator. While bringing the milk to a boil, sweeten it by stirring into each quart of milk 2 to 4 table-spoons of sugar or 3 to 6 tablespoons of honey. After the culture has been well stirred into the lukewarm milk, mix

* Directions might vary slightly for various incubators. Follow the at-tached instructions.

in (for each quart) 5 to 6 tablespoons of any kind of fruit syrup or preserve such as strawberry, raspberry or orange, or 3 to 4 tablespoons of chocolate syrup. Incubate and chill as in the above method.

Regulating the Taste

The taste of homemade yogurt may be regulated. For a mild flavor, chill as soon as the yogurt begins to thicken even slightly. (It will thicken further while chilling). For a tart flavor, incubate it longer.

Reasons for Failure

If the yogurt does not achieve its proper semisolid consistency and instead separates into curds and whey, there may be one or more reasons for the failure. The two primary reasons concern the incubation temperature and length of incubation. Either the temperature was too low or too high, or the yogurt was not incubated long enough. Another possible reason could be that when the culture was added to the hot milk it had not been cooled to lukewarm. Still another could be that adding the culture was forgotten. Or too much was added.

Do not discard any yogurt that has not thickened properly. It can be used as a starter.

Serving Yogurt

Plain or flavored yogurt may be served and eaten by itself as a snack or accompaniment to other foods. Plain yogurt may be sweetened with brown, white or powdered sugar, honey, maple syrup, marmalade, jam, chocolate sauce, fruit syrups or cinnamon and sugar. Sprinkle over or add to the plain yogurt any of the following: chopped olives, green onions, chives, watercress, dill, parsley, basil, paprika, garlic, chili or curry powder, nutmeg, cinnamon or such seeds as celery, mustard or sesame. Other ways of serving are given throughout the book.

Yogurt Cheese

Labanee or lebanie is an easily made Middle Eastern white cheese which can be served in a number of interesting ways. It can be a good substitute for cream cheese. To make it, stir some commercial or homemade yogurt and pour off any liquid. Put the yogurt in a bag, made with two or three layers of cheesecloth or muslin, and knot the top. Put in a colander or strainer in the sink and leave to drain three or four hours, or until most of the liquid or whey has drained off and the yogurt has thickened. Leave overnight to drain further. (In the Middle East the bag is sometimes hung on a nail with a pan underneath to catch the liquid.) Remove the cheese from the bag and season with salt. It should have a fairly thick consistency, similar to cream cheese. Because yogurt becomes tarter as it ages, the flavor of the cheese will be more piquant if the yogurt is several days old.

In the Middle East the cheese is served garnished with olive oil and eaten with flat Arabic bread and olives. It is also mixed with a combination of local spices, herbs and olive oil and served as a spread on bread. Another good spread can be made by mixing the cheese with olive oil and dried mint. Other suggestions include flavoring the cheese with minced chives, green onions, fresh herbs or seeds, such as sesame or mustard. The cheese may be also offered as a topping for or with fruit as the piquant flavor is a good contrast to that of fresh pears, apples, etc.

Yogurt Cheese Balls

In the Middle East yogurt cheese is shaped into balls, stored in olive oil and kept for several weeks. To make the balls, drain 1 quart of yogurt and make it into cheese according to the above directions. When the cheese is firm season with salt and mix well. Shape into smooth balls, about 1-inch in diameter. Leave overnight on a large plate in the refrigerator. Place in a large glass jar and cover with olive oil. Cover the jar. The balls will keep, unrefrigerated, for several weeks. Remove as needed. They may be eaten by themselves or mixed with a little oil, spices or herbs and used as a spread for bread.

Appetizers

Designed to whet the appetite, please the palate and attract the eye, cold and hot appetizers are inviting on any occasion. Alluring and flavorful appetizers made with yogurt are distinguished by their artful seasonings, interesting culinary contrasts and colorful garnishes. The varied creations contribute goodness and glamour to informal intimate social events, elegant cocktail receptions, bountiful buffets, light suppers, and can be starred as first courses of marvelous meals. The repertoire of these culinary delights is fascinating to explore and rewarding to savor.

The custom of serving tempting and satisfying foods at before the meal gatherings has long been traditional around the world. Near Easterners enjoyed olives, bits of cheese, unleavened bread, raw vegetables and yogurt for their *meze*. In ancient Egypt chick-peas, nuts, radishes and green onions were served with mugs of beer. The early Greeks relished stuffed grape leaves, savory meat balls and seafood as "provocatives to drinking." In ancient Rome gastronomes partook of a lengthy first course, *gustatio,* as they sipped their favorite honey-flavored wine.

In Europe each of the national cuisines developed an impressive array of artistic and imaginative appetizers. The Scandinavians created the smorgasbord, noted for its fish specialties and salads. In Russia a galaxy of toothsome native fare was called *zakuski*. The Austrians and Germans have long relished their varied and inviting *vorspeisen*. In France it became customary to serve a number of hors d'oeuvre as a prelude to luncheon. The Italian antipasto featured colorful and well seasoned fare. Whereas the *tapas* and *entremeses* of Spain include a wealth of mouth-watering dishes.

We Americans inherited many of these gastronomic treasures and have made them a part of our cuisine. But our creative cooks also devised some innovations such as dips and dunks, savory spreads and seafood cocktails to serve as first courses.

In itself, yogurt may be said to be one of the world's earliest appetizers. But its refreshing tart flavor and smooth texture are culinary assets which allow it to combine with other foods in versatile fashion, as demonstrated in this selection of taste tempting pre-meal attractions.

Avocado Yogurt Dip from California

Although avocados are of Central and South American origin and once grew wild, they are now widely cultivated in the United States. The majority of these flavorful fruits come from California and are sold in supermarkets throughout the country. Like yogurt, the avocado is not only a tasteful food but a nutritious one.

1 large ripe avocado	1 cup plain yogurt
2 tablespoons fresh lemon juice	1 garlic clove, crushed
	1 teaspoon chili powder
1 tablespoon grated onion	Salt, pepper to taste

Peel the avocado and remove the seed. Mash the pulp in a bowl and add the lemon juice. Mix well. Stir in the remaining ingredients and serve as a dip with corn or potato chips, crackers or raw vegetable fingers or wedges. Makes about 2 cups.

Russian Mushrooms on Toast

This flavorful *zakuska* is made in Russia traditionally with sour cream but yogurt is a good substitute. It may be served as an appetizer for a small group or as the first course of dinner.

1 cup minced green onions, with tops	⅓ cup butter or margarine
	2 teaspoons paprika

1 pound fresh mushrooms,
    cleaned and sliced
    thickly
2 teaspoons fresh lemon
    juice
2 tablespoons flour
2 cups plain yogurt, at
    room temperature

Salt, pepper to taste
4 slices rye or whole wheat
    bread, crusts removed,
    toasted and cut into
    triangles
Chopped fresh dill or
    parsley

Sauté the onions in the butter in a skillet or saucepan until tender. Add the paprika and cook 1 minute. Add the mushrooms and lemon juice and sauté for 4 minutes. Stir in the flour and blend well. Gradually add the yogurt and heat, stirring, until the mixture thickens. Season with salt and pepper and serve warm spooned over the toast triangles and garnished with the dill or parsley. Serves 4 to 6.

Hot Crabmeat Yogurt Canapes

One of America's most highly prized seafoods is delicate and flavorful crabmeat which is available either freshly cooked and iced, or canned. It is a great favorite for appetizers, prepared and served in interesting variety. Crabmeat and yogurt combine to make a good dip. This is a quick and easy recipe for imaginative canapes.

2 cups flaked crabmeat,
    cleaned
½ cup grated Parmesan
    cheese
1 teaspoon prepared
    mustard
½ cup (about) plain
    yogurt

Dash cayenne
Salt, pepper to taste
25 (about) small rounds of
    white bread
Chopped fresh parsley or
    paprika

Combine the crabmeat, cheese and mustard. Fold in the yogurt, enough to bind the mixture. Season with cayenne, salt and pepper. Spoon the crabmeat mixture onto the rounds of bread. Put under the broiler, about 3 inches from the heat, for 2 or 3 minutes. Decorate each one with parsley or paprika. Makes about 25.

Indian Rayta

Yogurt in one form or another is eaten daily in most Indian homes. One very good traditional dish is a refreshing combination of yogurt and fruits or vegetables and seasonings which is called *rayta* or *raita*. Generally it is served with the main meal, like a salad, as a cooling contrast to the hot curries. It can also be an appealing appetizer.

2 cups plain yogurt
½ cup minced onions
1 teaspoon minced green
    or red chili peppers
1 teaspoon ground cumin

Salt, pepper to taste
¼ cup finely chopped
    fresh coriander or
    parsley

Combine all the ingredients and chill. Serve in individual small bowls to be eaten with spoons or as a dip surrounded with crackers or bread. Serves 4 to 6.

Parisian Ham Yogurt Mousse

An elegant first course for a sit-down dinner or luncheon.

¼ cup cold water
1 envelope unflavored
    gelatine
¾ cup hot tomato juice
2 cups minced or ground
    cooked ham
½ cup finely chopped
    celery

¼ cup minced green
    pepper
½ teaspoon Worcestershire
    sauce
Salt, pepper to taste
1 cup plain yogurt
Lettuce leaves (optional)

Put the cold water in a medium sized bowl. Sprinkle the gelatine over it. Let stand 2 or 3 minutes. Add the hot tomato juice and stir until dissolved. Mix in the ham, celery, green pepper, Worcestershire, salt and pepper. Fold in the yogurt. Spoon into 6 individual small molds, custard cups or small glasses. Chill until firm. Unmold on lettuce leaves and serve garnished with a dollop of yogurt, if desired. Serves 6.

Cheese Yogurt Spread from Vienna

This recipe is adapted from a very popular Viennese appetizer called Liptauer or Liptói, a soft white cheese named after a province in Northern Hungary where it originated. Cottage cheese is a good substitute. The proportion of cheese and butter varies from cook to cook but the spread is always a well seasoned one. Yogurt adds further flavor to it.

1 cup creamed cottage
    cheese, drained
1/3 cup softened butter
1 tablespoon chopped
    drained capers
1 tablespoon prepared
    mustard

1 tablespoon minced onion
1 teaspoon anchovy paste
2 teaspoons paprika
1/2 cup plain yogurt
Salt, pepper to taste
1 teaspoon minced chives

Combine all the ingredients, except the chives, and mix well. Chill. Serve in a mound garnished with the chives and surrounded with pumpernickel slices or crackers. Makes 2 cups.

Continental Tuna Stuffed Tomatoes

These elegant and attractive stuffed tomatoes can be served as a luncheon or dinner first course; they are also appealing buffet fare.

6 *firm medium tomatoes*	2 *tablespoons chopped*
2 *cups drained and flaked*	*drained capers*
tuna fish	½ *teaspoon crushed dried*
4 *small green onions, with*	*rosemary*
tops, cleaned and	2 *cups plain yogurt*
minced	*Salt, pepper to taste*
¼ *cup finely chopped*	*Lettuce leaves (optional)*
green peppers	*Paprika*

Wash but do not peel the tomatoes. Cut out the stem end of each one. Cut each tomato into 6 sections by slicing from the stem end almost to the bottom. Gently pull apart the sections but do not separate them. Chill until ready to serve. In a bowl combine the remaining ingredients, except the lettuce and paprika. Chill. When ready to serve, arrange each tomato over a lettuce leaf on an individual small plate. Spoon the tuna-yogurt mixture into the tomato centers. Sprinkle the tops with paprika. Serves 6.

Rumanian Poor Man's Caviar

A very popular appetizer in the Balkan countries is a well seasoned eggplant dish which has been dubbed poor man's caviar. The term was probably applied because this was less expensive to serve than the tiny black pearls of sturgeon caviar. It is, nevertheless, an inviting creation to which yogurt adds extra flavor.

1 *medium eggplant,*	1 *cup plain yogurt*
washed	3 *tablespoons olive oil*
1 *cup minced onion*	2 *tablespoons fresh lemon*
2 *or 3 garlic cloves,*	*juice*
crushed or minced	½ *cup chopped fresh*
2 *medium tomatoes, peeled*	*parsley*
and chopped	*Salt, pepper to taste*

Prick the eggplant with a fork and place it on a cookie sheet. Bake in a preheated hot oven (400°F.) for about 50 minutes, or until tender. When cool enough to handle peel off the skins. Put the pulp in a bowl and drain off any liquid. Add the remaining ingredients and mix well. Chill. Before serving mix again and spoon off any excess liquid which may have accumulated during the chilling. Serve as a dip with crackers or crusty dark bread. Serves 6 to 8.

Melon and Ham with Yogurt Sauce

This is a very fine first course for a summer luncheon or dinner which can be easily prepared and attractively served. It is an adaptation of one of the most typical of Italian appetizer specialties. Serve wedges of chilled ripe melon with paper-thin slices of prosciutto (or other cured ham) laid over them, allowing 3 to 4 per person. Combine chilled plain yogurt, a touch of dry mustard, chopped chives or green onions, salt and pepper. Serve with the melon and ham to be spooned over them.

Mediterranean Artichoke Yogurt Hors D'Oeuvre

The aristocratic artichoke, widely cultivated and used in the Mediterranean countries, is further enhanced with this medley of colorful and flavorful foods.

2 packages (9 ounces) frozen artichoke hearts
1/4 cup mayonnaise
1 cup plain yogurt
4 to 6 anchovy fillets, minced
2 garlic cloves, crushed

1 tablespoon fresh lemon juice
1/2 teaspoon dried oregano
Pepper to taste
1 large tomato, washed and sliced
Black olives

Cook the artichokes according to the package directions. Drain and cool. Cut into halves lengthwise. Arrange on a large plate. When ready to serve combine the next seven ingredients and pour over the artichokes. Garnish with the tomato slices and olives. Serves 6.

Red Caviar and Yogurt Elegante

The combination of red caviar and yogurt is one that can be starred in several elegant and artistic appetizers. Actually the small red pearls are not technically caviar but roe taken from Pacific and Alaska Northwest salmon. Red caviar, however, is very tasty and its salty flavor is enhanced by that of yogurt. Included here are some suggestions for serving these two inviting foods.

1) Fill cleaned raw mushroom caps with red caviar and top with a little yogurt and sprig of dill.

2) Combine 1 cup plain yogurt, ½ cup red caviar, ¼ cup minced chives or green onions, 2 teaspoons fresh lemon juice, salt and pepper to make a dip for plain crackers or crusty white bread.

3) Fill slices of smoked salmon or other smoked fish with red caviar and roll them up. Serve each garnished with a dollop of yogurt and chopped fresh parsley. Serve lemon wedges with the appetizers.

4) Cut shelled hard-cooked eggs lengthwise. Mash the yolks and add grated onion, yogurt, salt and pepper. Fill the cavities of the egg with caviar and top with the mashed egg yolk-yogurt mixture.

Florida Citrus Fruit Cup

This delectable and attractive creation could be a good first course for a ladies' luncheon.

*2 cups diced grapefruit
   sections*   *2 cups diced orange
   sections*

2 cups diced fresh or
    canned pineapple
1 tablespoon fresh lime or
    lemon juice

1 carton (8 ounces) straw-
    berry or raspberry
    yogurt
Sugar to taste (optional)
Fresh mint leaves

Combine the fruits in a bowl and chill. Mix together the lime or lemon juice, yogurt and sugar, if desired, and chill. When ready to serve spoon the fruits into sherbet glasses or small bowls. Spoon the yogurt sauce over them. Garnish with the mint leaves. Serves 6.

New England Clam Yogurt Puffs

The clam, a well known and esteemed mollusk, has been an important food in New England ever since the colonists arrived. Clever cooks devised many delectable ways of preparing clams and they have become popular throughout the country. Canned clams are combined with cheese and yogurt to make these appealing canapes.

1 can (7 or 8 ounces)
    minced clams, drained
2 packages (3 ounces each)
    chive or plain cream
    cheese, softened
1 tablespoon grated onion
1 teaspoon Worcestershire
    sauce

Salt, pepper to taste
½ cup plain yogurt
30 (about) small rounds of
    white bread, toasted on
    one side, or crackers
Grated Parmesan cheese

Clean the clams and mince them as fine as possible. Combine with the cream cheese, onion, Worcestershire, salt and pepper. Fold in the yogurt. Mix well. Place a small spoonful on each of the rounds of bread. Sprinkle the top of each with grated Parmesan. Place under the broiler, about 3 inches from the heat, and broil 2 or 3 minutes, or until golden. Makes about 30.

Note: This mixture will also make a good dip if additional yogurt is added to it.

Party Cheese Ball from Holland

Either of two of the world's greatest cheeses, Edam and Gouda of Holland, can be used to make this attraction, superb for a party table.

3 cups grated Gouda or Edam cheese	*2 tablespoons chopped fresh parsley*
⅓ cup crumbled blue cheese	*½ teaspoon Worcestershire sauce*
2 tablespoons minced chives	*½ cup plain yogurt*
	½ cup chopped nuts

Combine the cheeses in a small bowl and beat until smooth. Add the chives, parsley and Worcestershire and beat again to thoroughly blend the ingredients. Fold in the yogurt. Cover and chill. Shape into a ball and roll in the nuts. Chill until ready to serve. Place on a plate surrounded with crackers. Makes about 3 cups.

German Filled Ham Cornets

In recent years the traditional German array of appetizers, *vorspeisen*, before foods, has been enhanced with the addition of many contemporary specialties such as this one. A good appetizer or first course.

1½ cups small curd cottage cheese	*2 tablespoons minced green onions, with tops*

1/3 *cup minced canned or*
    raw mushrooms
1 *tablespoon chopped fresh*
    parsley
Salt, pepper to taste

1/3 *cup plain yogurt*
12 *thin slices boiled ham,*
    cut into 4-inch squares
Paprika

Combine the cheese, onions, mushrooms, parsley, salt and pepper and mix well. Fold in the yogurt and chill. Roll the ham squares into cornets and fasten with toothpicks. Fill with the cheese-yogurt combination. Sprinkle the tops with paprika. Chill until ready to serve. Makes 12.

South of the Border Chili Dip

An easy to prepare dip flavored with seasonings which are typical ingredients in Mexico and our southwest.

1 *cup small or large curd*
    cottage cheese
1/2 *cup chili sauce*
1 *medium garlic clove,*
    crushed or minced

2 *to 3 teaspoons chili*
    powder
1/2 *teaspoon dried oregano*
Salt, pepper to taste
1 *cup plain yogurt*

Combine all the ingredients, except the yogurt, in a bowl and mix well. Fold in the yogurt. Cover and chill. Serve with corn chips. Makes about 2½ cups.

Turkish Fried Eggplant with Yogurt

In Turkey the eggplant is one of the most deeply appreciated vegetables and appears in interesting variations in the cuisine. Olive oil imparts a particularly desirable flavor to the colorful food and, if available, is preferable for frying the eggplant.

1 large eggplant, washed
Flour
Salt, pepper to taste
1 or 2 eggs, beaten
Fine dry bread crumbs

Oil for frying
1½ cups plain yogurt
2 garlic cloves, crushed
⅓ cup chopped fresh
    parsley

Remove the stem from the eggplant and cut crosswise into strips, about ⅛ inch thick. Dip into flour, seasoned with salt and pepper; then into beaten egg; and then into bread crumbs. Fry the slices, a few at a time, in heated oil in a skillet until golden and crisp on both sides. Drain on absorbent paper. Serve at once with the yogurt, garlic and parsley, seasoned with salt and pepper, spooned over the fried eggplant. Serves 6 to 8.

Yogurt Raw Vegetable Dip

Serve as a dip with such vegetables as cucumber fingers, carrot sticks, cauliflower flowerets, radishes, cherry tomatoes, celery and green or red sweet pepper strips.

2 cups plain yogurt
1 or 2 garlic cloves,
    crushed
2 tablespoons prepared
    mustard
⅓ cup chopped green

onions, with tops
2 tablespoons chopped
    drained capers
¼ cup minced fresh
    parsley
Salt, pepper to taste

Combine all the ingredients and mix well. Chill. Makes about 2¼ cups.

Pacific Salmon Piquant

Salmon has a pleasing flavor and is highly nutritious. It is caught in both the North Atlantic and Pacific oceans as well as in some fresh-water streams. The Pacific salmon, of which there are five species (king, red or sockeye, silver, pink and chum) are important commercially, particularly since most of the supply is canned. The majority of our canned salmon comes from Alaska, with Washington, Oregon and California contributing the remainder. This appealing appetizer is one of the many inventive dishes that can be made with salmon and yogurt.

1 can (1 pound) salmon, red or pink	1 cup plain yogurt
1 tablespoon grated onion	Salt, pepper to taste
1/4 teaspoon crumbled dried tarragon or rosemary	1 tablespoon drained red caviar
1/2 teaspoon grated lemon peel	Crackers or crusty white bread

Drain the salmon. Remove and discard the skin and bones. Mash the salmon and combine with the onion, tarragon and lemon peel. Fold in the yogurt and season with salt and pepper. Chill. When ready to serve spoon off any accumulated liquid. Shape into a mound on a plate. Garnish with the caviar and serve with crackers or pieces of white bread. Makes about 2 cups.

Note: Interesting appetizers can be made with this mixture by serving it on rounds of cucumber.

Low Calorie Dip or Spread

Weight watchers will enjoy this flavorful combination which can be easily made and attractively served.

1 box (eight ounces) skim-milk or creamed cottage cheese	2 tablespoons minced green onions, with tops, or chives
1 cup chopped fresh mushrooms	2 teaspoons fresh lemon juice

2 tablespoons chopped
    fresh dill or parsley
Salt, pepper to taste

½ to 1 cup plain yogurt
Paprika

Combine all the ingredients, except the paprika, and mix well. Use enough yogurt to make the desired thinness. Serve as a dip with raw vegetable pieces or as a spread for small rounds of pumpernickel or any other dark bread. Garnish with the paprika. Makes about 2½ to 3 cups.

Note: Use more yogurt for the dip than for the spread.

Near Eastern Cucumber Yogurt Appetizer

Throughout the Near East, from Greece to Iran, and also in the Balkans, a very popular appetizer is made with cucumbers and yogurt with the addition of other ingredients according to local preferences. Most often the inviting cool combination is flavored with dill, parsley or mint; lemon juice or vinegar; and garlic. One interesting variation, however, includes yellow or golden raisins; another, chopped nuts. Sometimes ice cubes are added to the appetizer just before it is served. This is one variation.

2 medium cucumbers,
    peeled, seeded and
    chopped finely
Salt
2 cups (about) plain
    yogurt
2 garlic cloves, crushed or
    minced

Juice of 1 medium lemon
2 teaspoons chopped fresh
    dill
Pepper to taste
2 tablespoons olive oil
1 tablespoon chopped fresh
    mint

Put the cucumbers in a colander or bowl and sprinkle with salt. Leave about 20 minutes. Drain off all the liquid. Combine the yogurt, garlic, lemon juice, dill and pepper.

Add the drained cucumber and mix well. Chill. Correct the seasoning. Serve sprinkled on the top with the oil and mint. Serve in small bowls as individual appetizers to be eaten with spoons or as a dip with Arabic bread or crackers. Serves 4 to 6.

Quick Creamy Onion Clam Dip

The ordinary onion has been taken for granted for so long that we sometimes do not appreciate its great contribution to our everyday cookery. "The cinderella of the kitchen" should be accorded more respect as our meals would be very dull without this versatile vegetable. Several appealing appetizers can be made with onions. This easy one is a combination of onion soup mix, made with dehydrated onions, yogurt and clams. It is a superb dip for any impromptu gathering and can be served with potato chips, corn chips or crackers.

1 envelope (1⅜ ounces)
   onion soup mix
2 cups plain yogurt
½ cup drained minced
   clams

¼ cup grated Parmesan
   cheese
Paprika

Combine the ingredients, except the paprika, and mix well. Chill. Serve in a bowl garnished with the paprika. Makes about 2½ cups.

Persian Spinach Borani

In Persia, or Iran as it is known today, a traditional appetizer is a flavorful combination made with yogurt, a vegetable and seasonings. The chilled mixture is eaten with bread as a first course but may be served also as a dip with crackers, or as a salad or accompaniment to meat or poultry. A similar dish can be made using raw cucumbers, cooked mushrooms, beets or eggplant, instead of the spinach.

2 packages (10 ounces each) frozen chopped spinach	2 tablespoons butter or vegetable oil
1 large onion, finely chopped	1 cup (about) plain yogurt
1 or 2 garlic cloves, crushed	½ teaspoon ground cinnamon
	Salt, pepper to taste

Cook the spinach according to the package directions and drain. Press out all the liquid and chop very finely or whirl in a blender. Set aside. Sauté the onion and garlic in the butter in a saucepan until tender. Mix in the spinach and sauté about 1 minute to blend the flavors. Add the yogurt, cinnamon, salt and pepper and remove from the heat. Chill. Serves 8.

Note: More yogurt may be added to the mixture if a thinner consistency is desired.

Shrimp Cocktail with Yogurt Sauce

America's very popular first course, shrimp cocktail, takes on a new flavor when the sauce is made with yogurt which marries well with shrimp.

1 cup plain yogurt	Salt, pepper to taste
¼ cup mayonnaise	1 pound cooked, shelled and deveined medium shrimp
¼ cup ketchup	
1 tablespoon minced chives or green onions	
1 tablespoon prepared horseradish, drained	Chopped lettuce or lettuce leaves
Few drops tabasco or hot sauce	Lemon wedges

Combine the yogurt, mayonnaise, ketchup, chives, horseradish, tabasco, salt and pepper and chill. When ready to serve, arrange the shrimp, dividing evenly, on chopped lettuce or lettuce leaves in 6 short-stemmed glasses or small bowls. Spoon the yogurt sauce over them. Serve a lemon wedge with each one. Serves 6.

Note: The shrimp, arranged on lettuce, and covered with the sauce, may be served on a platter or in a large bowl, if desired.

Copenhagen Open-Faced Sandwiches

For many visitors to captivating Copenhagen the most inviting gastronomic pleasures are the delectable and artistic open-faced sandwiches called *smørrebrød*, buttered bread. The Danes eat them daily for luncheon or as snacks, and they are prepared and sold in great variety. One restaurant has a menu with over 175 different kinds. The well buttered white or dark firm bread has toppings made with poultry, seafood, meats, eggs or vegetables, or a combination of them, and handsome garnishes. Yogurt is not a traditional Danish ingredient but its tart flavor and smooth consistency adds to the appeal of these sandwiches. Included here are three easy to prepare suggestions which can be served as appetizers, as first courses, or as luncheon or supper entrees. Serve and eat with knives and forks.

1) Spread slices of firm white bread generously with butter. Place a bibb lettuce leaf on each slice. Cover with a combination of diced cooked seafood (shrimp, lobster, crabmeat, salmon or tuna), diced celery, ketchup, yogurt, salt and pepper. Garnish with slivers of green pepper.

2) Spread slices of rye bread with butter and mustard. Place a slice of thin cooked ham on each bread slice. Cover with a combination of chopped hard-cooked egg, relish, minced onion, yogurt, salt and pepper. Garnish with paprika.

3) Spread slices of firm white or dark bread with butter and mayonnaise. Place a lettuce leaf on each slice and top

with tomato slices. Add a large spoonful of chopped cucumber, minced sweet pickle, yogurt, salt and pepper. Garnish with chopped fresh dill or parsley.

Herbed Yogurt Seafood Dip

An excellent party dip to serve with chilled cooked shrimp, crab legs, cubes of cooked lobster, raw oysters and/or clams.

1 cup mayonnaise	*¾ cup minced fresh herbs*
1 cup plain yogurt	*(parsley, basil, dill,*
½ cup minced green	*tarragon)*
onions, with tops	*Salt, pepper to taste*
1 tablespoon fresh lemon	*Paprika*
juice	

Combine all the ingredients, except the paprika, and chill. Serve garnished with paprika and surrounded with the seafood. Makes about 2½ cups.

Vegetable Pachadi from India

A well-seasoned yogurt vegetable appetizer, called *pachadi* in Southern India, may be served as a first course in small bowls and eaten with spoons or as a dip with crackers or Indian unleavened bread, *chapati*. It may also be served as an accompaniment to curry.

1 medium onion, finely	*1 to 2 teaspoons chili*
chopped	*powder*
1 garlic clove, crushed	*2 medium tomatoes, peeled*
2 tablespoons vegetable oil	*and chopped*
1 to 2 tablespoons curry	*1 teaspoon minced hot*
powder	*green chilies*
	(optional)

1 cup diced cucumber
2 cups plain yogurt
Salt, pepper to taste

2 tablespoons chopped
fresh coriander or
parsley

Sauté the onion and garlic in the oil in a skillet until tender. Add the curry and chili powders and cook for 1 minute. Remove from the heat and mix with the remaining ingredients. Serves 6 to 8.

Soups

Among the world's gastronomic delights the rich repertoire of savory soups is particularly notable. Whether termed a bisque, *brodo*, bouillon, broth, chowder, consommé, *čorba*, potage, purée, *sopa* or *zuppa*, each is fascinating to prepare and delightful to enjoy. Yogurt imparts an attractive flavor and appearance and nutrient richness both to the light and aristocratic and the hearty and humble varieties.

Soup is superb for every occasion. Elegant ones, designed to stimulate the appetite, are appealing first courses. Substantial creations may be served as one-dish meals. Soups are excellent for brunches, luncheons, suppers or late-evening parties. Orientals enjoy soup for breakfast, as a between meal snack, and to refresh the palate after dining. Some Europeans and Near Easterners drink soups in the wee hours of the morning as a restorative after a night of revelry.

The saga of soup dates back to the beginnings of cookery when ancient man discovered the idea of filling an empty animal skin bag with meat, bones, liquid and the hot stones which cooked the mixture. With the invention of clay containers the ingredients became more varied and were simmered over direct heat. Thus was created the first *pot au feu* or pot on the fire.

The initial literary reference to a soup is found in the Bible where in Genesis we can read that Esau sold his birthright to his brother Jacob for "a pottage of lentils." Over the centuries cooks, utilizing the available bounty of land and sea, created a galaxy of national favorites, each prepared and flavored according to local tastes. They bequeathed us a wealthy heritage of fascinating variety.

To soups we are indebted for the establishment of the first restaurant and the word itself. In 1765 an enterprising Parisian soup vendor began advertising his sole menu item as "magical" *restaurants* (re-storatives or pick-me-ups) .

Yogurt was probably first prepared as a soup in the Near East when such flavorings as garlic, onions and herbs were mixed with it. During the summer it was eaten cold and in winter months enjoyed hot. In each of the cuisines of southeastern Europe and the Middle East yogurt became a popular ingredient in a variety of fascinating soups. The Bulgarians laced a hearty lamb-rice combination with the cultured milk and the Iranians used it to impart an appealing flavor to an ancient classic soup made with a variety of vegetables and herbs.

The possibilities for utilizing yogurt in soups are limitless. It is a marvelous substitute for sour cream in traditional dishes of Central European and Northern Russian cuisines. Fortunately, it mixes well with the spicy seasonings so popular in Latin America and Southeast Asia. Yogurt makes the modern easy-to-prepare soup preparations more elegant and nourishing.

A great deal of pleasure can be derived from the cookery of intri-cate or simple soups but there is also an excitement in serving these dishes. A light and refreshing first course can be attractively presented in fine china soup bowls or handsome cups. Nourishing and hearty thick soups in handsome tureens are perfect adornments for buffets or informal dinner parties.

This cosmopolitan collection of yogurt soup recipes includes some classic recipes and some innovative suggestions for preparing this fascinating food in dishes for family and company meals. On all oc-casions when savoring any of them it might be well to remember the words of the skilled chef Escoffier: "Soup puts the heart at ease, calms down the violence of hunger, eliminates the tension of the day, and awakens and refines the appetite."

Lentil Yogurt Soup Indienne

In the Mediterranean and Middle Eastern countries one of the most highly prized foods has long been the lentil. Little wonder as it is extremely nutritious and richer in iron than any other legume. The lentil, called *dal*, is grown in great variety in India and appears in many dishes. This soup features another favorite Indian food, yogurt.

2 cups dried lentils,
   washed and picked
   over
2 medium onions, peeled
   and chopped
2 or 3 garlic cloves,
   crushed
1/4 cup vegetable shortening or oil

2 teaspoons ground
   turmeric
1 teaspoon chili powder
1/4 teaspoon ground
   coriander (optional)
8 cups water
Salt, pepper to taste
2 cups plain yogurt

Prepare the lentils according to the package directions. They may or may not require soaking. Sauté the onions and garlic in the oil in a large kettle until tender. Add the turmeric, chili powder and coriander, and cook, stirring, for 1 minute. Add the lentils and water and season with salt and pepper. Bring to a boil. Lower the heat and simmer, covered, for 1½ hours, or until the lentils are cooked. Gently stir in the yogurt and leave on the stove just long enough to heat through. Serves 8.

Jellied Yogurt Consommé

Serve this cold soup in attractive cups or glasses with creative sandwiches for a company luncheon.

4 cups chicken broth
2 envelopes unflavored
   gelatine
1/8 teaspoon crumbled
   dried basil

1/8 teaspoon crumbled
   dried thyme
Salt, pepper to taste
1 cup plain yogurt
2 tablespoons dry sherry

Put 1 cup of the cold chicken broth in a bowl and sprinkle the gelatine over it. When soft pour into a large saucepan. Add the remaining broth, basil, thyme, salt and pepper. Stir over low heat until dissolved. Heat, stirring, until just to the boiling point. Stir in the yogurt and sherry and remove from the heat. Cool and then chill until firm. Cut or break up with a fork into small cubes. Serve in chilled cups or bowls garnished with watercress or parsley, if desired. Serves 4 to 6.

Near Eastern Cucumber Yogurt Refresher

A versatile creation eaten as an appetizer, soup or type of salad, is made with yogurt, cucumbers and other foods. Its origin is lost in history, but the dish is a national favorite from the Balkans to Iran and is called turquoise or *cacik* in Turkey, *tarator* in Bulgaria, *tzatziki* in Greece and *mast na khiar* in Iran. It is a very good summer soup eaten cold but may be heated gently and served hot.

4 cups plain yogurt
2 garlic cloves, crushed
2 medium cucumbers,
    peeled and chopped
½ cup chopped walnuts
1 tablespoon wine vinegar

Salt, white pepper to taste
2 tablespoons olive or vege-
    table oil (optional)
1 tablespoon minced fresh
    mint (optional)

Beat the yogurt smooth in a large bowl. Add the garlic, cucumbers, walnuts, vinegar, salt and pepper and mix well. Chill until ready to serve. To serve, spoon into small bowls or cups and garnish with a little oil and mint, if desired. Serves 4 to 6.

Blender Broccoli Yogurt Soup

A soup such as this velvety one can be easily and quickly made in a blender and served either hot or cold. Designed to stimulate the appetite, it is a good first course.

1 package (10 ounces) fro-
    zen chopped broccoli
1 medium garlic clove
2 cups chicken broth or 2
    chicken bouillon cubes
    and 2 cups water

½ teaspoon dried basil
Dash cayenne pepper
Salt, pepper to taste
¾ cup plain yogurt

Cook the broccoli in a little water for about 8 minutes, or until tender. Cool. Spoon into a blender container. Add the remaining ingredients, except the yogurt, and blend, covered, about 10 seconds, or until smooth. Add the yogurt and blend for about a second. Chill. Serves 4.

Note: This soup may also be heated and served hot. Blend all the ingredients, except the yogurt. Pour into a saucepan and bring just to a boil. Lower the heat and stir in the yogurt. Leave on the stove just long enough to heat through.

Polish Barley Vegetable Pot with Yogurt

Barley was one of the world's first important foods, used to make porridges, breads and even beer, and quickly spread from the Middle East to many lands where it became an important staple. In Europe barley has long been a vital ingredient in many national soups, especially those of the central and northern countries. The grain has an appealing nutty flavor, is high in nutritive value and can be prepared in interesting variation. This is a nourishing, hearty soup, good for a winter supper.

½ to ¾ *pound soup bone with meat*

2 *medium carrots, scraped and diced*

2 *medium onions, peeled and diced*

1 *tablespoon chopped celery leaves*

2 *tablespoons chopped fresh parsley*

3 *dried mushrooms (optional)*

6 *peppercorns, bruised*

Salt to taste

½ *cup pearl barley*

3 *tablespoons butter*

3 *medium potatoes, peeled and diced*

3 *tablespoons chopped dill*

1 *cup plain yogurt*

Put the soup bone with meat and 8 cups of water in a large kettle. Bring to a boil. Skim well. Add the carrots, onions, celery leaves, parsley, mushrooms, peppercorns and salt. Lower the heat and cook slowly, covered, for 1½ hours. Meanwhile, put the barley and 3 cups of water in a saucepan. Cook slowly, covered, until tender, about 1¼ hours. Stir in the butter. When cooked, remove the kettle of soup from the heat and take out the soup bone and meat and mushrooms. Cut the meat from the bone. Discard any gristle and dice the meat. Dice the mushrooms. Return the meat and the mushrooms to the soup. Add the potatoes and continue to cook until the ingredients are tender, about 25 minutes. Mix in the cooked barley. Correct the seasoning. Add the dill and yogurt. Leave over the heat just long enough to warm the ingredients. Serves 8 to 10.

Tomato Yogurt Chiller

An attractive and appealing first-course soup for a ladies' luncheon.

2 cans (1 pound each) to-
    matoes, undrained
	1 tablespoon chopped fresh
	    parsley

4 green onions, with tops, minced	¼ teaspoon dried basil
1 teaspoon sugar	2 cups plain yogurt Salt, pepper to taste

Purée the tomatoes in an electric blender or put through a sieve or food mill. Mix with the remaining ingredients and chill for 3 or 4 hours. Serves 6.

Potage aux Herbes

Since earliest times aromatic plants called herbs have been widely utilized to impart desirable flavors to our foods. In Europe cooks created some interesting soups made with *herbs potageres*, pot herbs and vegetable greens, such as lettuce, sorrel, spinach, sea kale and purslane. Combined with yogurt they make a healthy and surprisingly delightful light *potage*.

2 tablespoons butter or
    margarine
⅓ cup chopped chives or
    green onions
1 cup shredded lettuce
½ cup chopped sorrel or
    spinach

½ cup chopped watercress
¼ cup chopped fresh
    parsley
6 cups beef bouillon
1 teaspoon sugar
Salt, pepper to taste
1 cup plain yogurt

Melt the butter in a heavy saucepan and sauté the chives in it until tender. Add the lettuce, sorrel or spinach, watercress and parsley. Simmer, covered, for 10 minutes. Add the beef bouillon, sugar, salt and pepper and simmer, covered, 30 minutes longer. Stir occasionally. Add the yogurt and leave on the stove long enough to heat through. Serves 6 to 8.

Yugoslavian Lamb Rice Čorba with Yogurt

In Yugoslavia holiday and special family meals are celebrated with steaming bowls of čorba, soup, made of lamb, rice, and yogurt. This is one variation which is particularly flavorful because the medley of ingredients is slowly cooked together. It is a hearty and healthy soup.

2 pounds breast of lamb,
    cut into large pieces
2 tablespoons butter or
    margarine
1 large onion, peeled and
    chopped
1 tablespoon paprika
Salt, pepper to taste
2½ quarts water

½ cup uncooked rice
2 packages (10 ounces
    each) frozen chopped
    spinach
2 tablespoons chopped
    fresh parsley
1 cup plain yogurt
2 tablespoons chopped
    fresh dill

Brown the lamb pieces in the butter in a large kettle. Push aside and add the onions. Sauté until tender. Stir in the paprika, salt and pepper and cook several seconds. Add the water and bring to a boil. Skim. Lower the heat and cook slowly, covered, for 2 hours. Skim again. Add the rice, spinach and parsley and cook about 25 minutes longer, or until the ingredients are tender. Take out the pieces of lamb and cut off the lean meat. Discard the fat and bones. Return the pieces of lamb to the soup. Combine the yogurt and dill and stir into the soup. Leave on the stove long enough to heat through. Serves 8 to 10.

Potage Parmentier with Yogurt

Antoine-Auguste Parmentier, a French horticulturist, worked tirelessly during the 18th century to have the despised New World potato accepted in Europe as a valuable and economical food. Thus any dish named Parmentier means that it includes potatoes.

4 medium leeks, white parts and 1 inch of the green, washed and sliced, or 3 medium onions, sliced
4 tablespoons butter or margarine

4 medium potatoes, peeled and diced
6 cups chicken broth or water
Salt, pepper to taste
1 cup plain yogurt
2 tablespoons chopped chives or green onions

Sauté the leeks or onions in 2 tablespoons of butter in a large saucepan or kettle over low heat until tender. Add the potatoes, broth, salt and pepper and bring to a boil. Lower the heat and cook slowly, covered, until tender, about 20 minutes. Put through a food mill or sieve, or whirl in a blender until smooth. Return to the saucepan. Add the yogurt and remaining 2 tablespoons of butter. Correct the seasoning. Serve garnished with the chives. Serves 4 to 6.

Circassian Vegetable Yogurt Soup

A long time ago the Circassians, a name given to all the independent tribes of the Caucasus in southern Russia, introduced many of their favorite dishes to their neighbors in the Middle East. Many of them, such as this soup, were flavored with their favorite yogurt and are still enjoyed in these lands.

1 beef soup bone
Salt, pepper to taste
1 medium bay leaf
1½ quarts water
1 large onion, peeled and
*   chopped*
⅓ cup uncooked rice

1 cup each of diced carrots,
*   cut-up green beans and*
*   green peas*
2 cups tomato juice
½ teaspoon dried oregano
*   or thyme*
1 teaspoon paprika
1 cup plain yogurt

Put the soup bone, salt, pepper, bay leaf and water in a large heavy kettle. Bring to a boil and skim. Lower the heat and cook slowly, covered, for 1½ hours. Skim again. Add the onion, rice, vegetables, tomato juice, oregano and paprika. Continue to cook slowly, covered, for about 30 minutes, or until the meat, rice and vegetables are tender. Remove the soup bone and bay leaf. Add the yogurt and leave on the heat long enough to warm through. Serves 10 to 12.

Avocado Yogurt Summer Soup

Serve this soup for a special summer luncheon or dinner either outdoors or inside.

1 large or 2 small avocados
1 teaspoon salt
1 garlic clove, crushed
2 tablespoons fresh lemon
*   juice*

¼ cup minced green
*   onions, with tops*
½ to 1 teaspoon chili
*   powder*
3 cups chicken broth
1½ cups plain yogurt

Cut the avocado or avocados into halves; remove seeds and skin. Whirl in a blender or purée with a fork; add the next five ingredients. Mix well and turn into a saucepan. Gradually add the chicken broth and heat to the boiling point. Stir in the yogurt and remove from the heat. Cool and chill until ready to serve. Serves 4 to 6.

Impromptu Yogurt Company Soups

Included here are four suggestions for making imaginative company soups by combining canned condensed soups, yogurt and one or two other foods. Each can be easily and quickly prepared.

I. Combine 2 cans (10½ ounces each) condensed cream of mushroom soup, 1 soup can milk, 1 soup can plain yogurt, and a dash of nutmeg. Heat gently. Serve garnished with chopped watercress. Serves 6.

II. Saute ¼ cup chopped green onions in 2 tablespoons butter or margarine until soft. Add 2 cans (10½ ounces each) condensed chicken soup with rice, 1 soup can water, 1 soup can plain yogurt and 2 tablespoons chopped fresh parsley. Heat gently. Serves 6.

III. Combine 1 can (11¼ ounces) condensed green pea soup and 1 can (10¾ ounces) condensed tomato soup, 1 cup water, 1 cup plain yogurt and 2 teaspoons curry powder. Heat gently. Serves 6.

IV. Combine 1 can (10½ ounces) condensed cream of celery soup, 1 can (10½ ounces) condensed cream of asparagus soup, 1 soup can milk, 1 soup can plain yogurt, ¼ cup chopped watercress, and ¼ teaspoon dried basil. Heat gently. Serves 6.

Continental Mushroom Yogurt Creme

Two marvelous and magical foods, mushrooms and yogurt, are combined in this rich cream soup which is an excellent first course for a very special dinner party.

1 pound fresh mushrooms
4 green onions with tops,
    minced
1/4 cup butter or margarine
2 tablespoons flour
1 quart chicken broth or
    beef bouillon

1/2 teaspoon dried rose-
    mary, crumbled
Salt, pepper to taste
1 1/2 cups plain yogurt
Minced chives

Wash the mushrooms quickly or wipe them with wet paper toweling to remove any dirt. Cut off any tough stem ends. Slice from the round sides through the stems. Sauté the onions in the butter in a large saucepan until tender. Add the mushroom slices and sauté 4 minutes. Stir in the flour; blend well. Gradually add the broth or bouillon, stirring while adding. Mix in the rosemary, salt and pepper. Simmer, covered, for 10 minutes. Add the yogurt and leave on the stove long enough to heat through. Serve garnished with the chives. Serves 4 to 6.

Bulgarian Meatball Rice Soup with Yogurt

A favorite Bulgarian dish, this nourishing and refreshing soup could be served to a group of men who gather for an evening get-together or after returning from an afternoon of outdoor sports. Offer a plate of hearty cheese sandwiches with it.

3/4 pound lean ground beef
1 small onion, minced
1 tablespoon chopped fresh
    dill
2 eggs, beaten
1 garlic clove, crushed
Salt, pepper to taste

Flour
6 cups beef bouillon
1/3 cup uncooked rice
Juice of 1/2 lemon
2 tablespoons chopped
    fresh parsley
1 cup plain yogurt

Combine the ground beef, onion, dill, 1 egg, garlic, salt and pepper in a large bowl. Mix until the ingredients are well combined. Shape into small balls, about 1 inch in diameter. Dredge in flour and set aside. Bring the beef bouillon to a boil. Drop in the meatballs and rice. Lower the heat and cook slowly, covered, until the rice is tender and the meatballs are cooked, about 25 minutes. Mix together the lemon juice and remaining egg. Stir in the parsley. Add some of the hot broth, beating constantly while adding, and return to the soup. Cook slowly, stirring, until well blended and thickened. Serve with a spoonful of yogurt on top of each bowl of soup. Serves 6 to 8.

Note: This may be partially prepared beforehand. Add the lemon juice, egg and yogurt just before serving.

Weight Watchers Mushroom Yogurt Soup

Two favorite foods which are low in calories, mushrooms and yogurt, are combined with seasonings to make this refreshing soup. Good as a snack or a first course.

1 medium onion, chopped	*1 tablespoon fresh lemon*
2 tablespoons peanut or	*juice*
vegetable oil	*⅛ teaspoon nutmeg*
½ pound fresh mush-	*Salt, pepper to taste*
rooms, thinly sliced	*4 cups beef consommé*
	2 cups plain yogurt

Sauté the onion in the oil until tender. Add the mushrooms and lemon juice and sauté 3 minutes. Stir in the remaining ingredients and heat gently. Serve at once. Serves 6.

Rumanian Onion Tomato Ciorba

The cuisine of Rumania is particularly interesting because it has delightful resemblances to Slavic, Balkan and Hungarian dishes but is the only Eastern European country to have a Latin influence, acquired when it was an outpost of Imperial Rome. This soup is typical of the inviting fare as it is rich in ingredients and flavor but deftly seasoned and light. Serve as a first course or with warm corn bread for luncheon or supper.

4 cups sliced onions	Salt, pepper to taste
2 garlic cloves, crushed	2 tablespoons chopped
1/4 cup butter or margarine	fresh dill
6 cups tomato juice	1 cup plain yogurt
1/2 teaspoon celery seed	

Sauté the onions and garlic in the butter in a large saucepan until the onions are soft. Add the tomato juice, celery seed, salt and pepper and simmer, covered, for 30 minutes. Stir in the dill and yogurt and leave on the stove long enough to heat through. Serves 6 to 8.

Turkish Chicken Rice Soup

Čorbasi, the rich soups of Turkey, are some of the world's best as they are flavorful combinations enriched with such excellent foods as herbs, vegetables and yogurt. This fine example, gentle and appealing, would be a good first course for a company meal.

6 cups chicken broth	2 tablespoons butter or
Salt, pepper to taste	margarine
2 cups plain yogurt	2 tablespoons chopped
1 tablespoon flour	fresh mint or parsley
2 egg yolks, well beaten	

Bring the broth to a boil in a saucepan. Season with salt and pepper. Lower the heat. Combine the yogurt, flour and beaten egg yolks in a small bowl and stir about 3 tablespoons of the hot broth into the mixture. Mix well and return to the broth. Cook over low heat, stirring, about 1 or 2 minutes. Add the butter and mint and serve. Serves 6 to 8.

Spring Fresh Asparagus Soup with Yogurt

One of the first signs and great delights of spring is fresh asparagus. In Western Europe the thick white stalks are highly prized but in our country green asparagus is generally preferred. Asparagus is a taste treat, goes well with other foods, and is a good source of vitamin A. The combination of this delectable vegetable and yogurt makes an aristocratic soup for a holiday or special meal.

1 pound green asparagus	*2 tablespoons flour*
Water	*2 egg yolks, lightly beaten*
2 teaspoons sugar	*Freshly ground pepper and*
Salt to taste	*grated nutmeg to taste*
1 cup plain yogurt	*3 tablespoons chopped*
2 tablespoons softened butter	*fresh parsley*

Trim off the scales and any tough stalk ends from the asparagus. Wash well and cut into 1-inch pieces, reserving the tips. Put 5 cups of water in a kettle and bring to a boil. Add the asparagus pieces and sugar and season lightly with salt. Lower the heat and cook slowly, covered, about 12 minutes, or until the asparagus is tender. Cook the tips separately in salted boiling water to cover until tender. Drain the tips and set aside. Put the cooked asparagus pieces and liquid through a sieve or whirl in a blender until smooth. Heat in a saucepan. Add the yogurt. Combine the butter and flour until smooth and form into tiny balls. Drop into the soup and cook slowly, stirring, until thickened. Spoon some of the hot mixture to combine with the egg yolks. Mix well and return to the kettle. Add the asparagus tips, pepper and nutmeg. Season with salt. Leave on the stove only a few minutes, stirring. Serve garnished with the parsley. Serves 6.

Note: The soup may also be prepared with frozen asparagus spears. Cook according to the package directions.

Shrimp Yogurt Bisque Elegante

A bisque is perfect for a ladies bridge luncheon as it can be prepared beforehand and is attractive and delectable. Serve with warm small rolls and a dainty salad.

¼ cup butter or margarine
1 medium onion, minced
2 tablespoons minced
    green pepper
2 tablespoons flour
2 tablespoons tomato paste
2 cups light cream or milk

½ teaspoon dried basil or
    thyme
Salt, pepper to taste
¾ pound cleaned, cooked
    shrimp
2 cups plain yogurt
Lemon slices
Chopped chives

Melt the butter in a saucepan and add the onion and green pepper. Sauté until tender. Mix in the flour and cook, stirring, about 1 minute. Add the tomato paste and cream and cook slowly, stirring, until the sauce becomes thickened and smooth. Add the basil, salt and pepper and cook slowly about 5 minutes. Mix in the shrimp and add the yogurt. Leave on the stove long enough to heat through. Serve garnished with the lemon slices and chives. Serves 6.

Persian Yogurt Ashe

The Persians, or Iranians as they are now called, are fond of rich soups, laced with yogurt and well flavored with such favorite seasonings as green onions, parsley and mint, which they call *ashes*. This would be a delightful luncheon dish to serve with fancy sandwiches. The soup has an appealing lemon-like flavor.

¾ pound ground beef
3 tablespoons grated or
    minced onion
Salt, pepper to taste

1 quart plain yogurt
4 cups water
2 tablespoons flour
2 medium eggs, beaten

¼ cup uncooked rice	⅓ cup chopped fresh
⅓ cup minced green on-	parsley
ions, with tops	2 teaspoons dried mint
	(optional)

Combine the ground beef, onion, salt and pepper and mix well. Shape into tiny meatballs and set aside. Heat the yogurt in a large saucepan or kettle. Combine ½ cup of water, the flour and eggs in a small bowl and mix well. Add with the rice to the heated yogurt and mix with a whisk or fork to blend the ingredients. Stir in the remaining water. Cook over a very low fire, stirring constantly, until the mixture thickens. Add the meatballs and continue to cook slowly, covered, for about 20 minutes, or until the rice and meatballs are cooked. Stir in the green onions, parsley and mint and remove from the heat. Serve at once. Serves 6 to 8.

Russian Borsch

This well known soup, called *borsch, borscht, barszcz* or *bartsch,* was introduced to Eastern Europe by the Tartars in ancient times and became a national favorite in several countries. There are many varieties of the soup and within Russia they differ not only from region to region but family to family. Some are substantial; others light. Beets are always included and generally there are other vegetables. In the north sour cream is added but in the southern regions yogurt is the favorite flavoring. This is a hearty version of *borsch.*

8 medium-sized beets	2 medium onions, peeled
2 pounds lean beef (chuck	and chopped
or stew meat)	3 cups coarsely chopped
1 bay leaf	cabbage
6 peppercorns, bruised	6 medium fresh or canned
2 sprigs parsley	tomatoes, peeled and
2 medium carrots, scraped	chopped
and sliced thinly	Salt to taste

½ cup vinegar   1 cup plain yogurt
1 tablespoon sugar

Wash the beets and cook 7 of them, unpeeled, in salted
water to cover until tender, 30 to 40 minutes. Peel and cut
into julienne. Put the meat and 2½ quarts of water in a
kettle and bring to a boil. Skim well. Add the bay leaf, peppercorns, parsley, carrots and onions. Cook slowly, covered,
for 1 hour. Add the cooked beets, cabbage and tomatoes.
Cook about 45 minutes, or until the ingredients are cooked.
Take out the meat and cut into small pieces. Return to the
kettle. Remove and discard the bay leaf and peppercorns.
Season with salt. Peel and grate the remaining beet. Place
in a saucepan with 1 cup of the soup liquid, the vinegar and
sugar. Bring to a boil. Stir into the soup. Put a spoonful of
yogurt into each soup bowl and pour the soup over it. Serves
12. Excellent when reheated.

Tasty Tuna Kale Supper Soup from the South

Kale, a variety of cabbage, is unfortunately often overlooked as a vegetable. The dark bluish green leaves should
be highly prized as they have a high vitamin content, are inexpensive and are in ample supply. Kale or *kail* has long
been a staple winter food in Scotland and was probably introduced by Scots to our southeastern states where it also
became favorite fare. The combination of kale and tuna,
flavored with yogurt, results in an unusual and nourishing
one-dish meal for a family supper.

1 package (10 ounces) fro-   1 soup can milk
    zen kale   2 cups plain yogurt
½ cup chopped onion   1 can (6½ to 7 ounces)
2 tablespoons butter or   tuna, drained and
    margarine   flaked
1 can (10½ ounces) con-   2 tablespoons chopped
    densed cream of celery   fresh parsley
    soup   Few drops tabasco

Cook the kale according to the package directions. Sauté the onion in the butter until tender. Add the kale and remaining ingredients and heat gently. Serves 6.

Vegetarian Bean Yogurt Party Pot

This is a hearty thick soup made with pinto beans, corn and macaroni, well seasoned with flavorings that are favorites in Mexico and our southwest. Yogurt blends beautifully with the hot chili powder, garlic and spices and gives the soup an interesting and different flavor. Serve with a tray of raw vegetables and warm corn bread or muffins for an early or late evening party.

1 pound dried pinto beans	seed
2 quarts water	1 cup tomato sauce
2 teaspoons salt	Pepper to taste
1 large onion, chopped	3 cups tomato juice
1 or 2 garlic cloves, crushed	1½ cups frozen corn niblets
2 tablespoons vegetable oil	1½ cups elbow macaroni
1 tablespoon chili powder	2 cups plain yogurt
½ teaspoon ground oregano	2 tablespoons parsley flakes
½ teaspoon ground cumin	½ cup minced green pepper

Put the beans and water in a large kettle and bring to a boil. Boil for 2 minutes. Remove from the heat. Let stand, covered, for 1 hour. Return to the heat and add the salt. Mix well and bring to a boil. Lower the heat and cook slowly, covered, for 1 hour. While the beans are cooking sauté the onion and garlic in the oil in a small skillet or saucepan until tender. Stir in the chili power, oregano and cumin. Cook for 1 minute. Add the tomato sauce. Season with salt and pepper. Cook about 1 minute, long enough to blend the flavors. When the beans have cooked for 1 hour, stir the onion-tomato mixture into the pot. Continue the slow cooking for another 30 minutes. Add the tomato juice, corn and macaroni and cook about 15 minutes longer, or until the vegetables and macaroni are tender. Stir in the yogurt and parsley and leave on the stove long enough to heat through. Serve in a large tureen or pot with the green pepper sprinkled over the soup. Serves 12.

one-half dozen eggs

Egg and Cheese Dishes

A wealth of imaginative culinary creations can be made with two of man's earliest and most versatile foods, eggs and cheese. Either by themselves, together, or combined with other ingredients they are superb for around the clock dining and cookery. Fortunately they mix most agreeably with yogurt and provide us with a fascinating repertoire of innovative and nourishing fare for all occasions.

One of nature's almost perfect foods, the egg is highly valued for the important amount and high quality of protein it contains. Eggs also provide us with considerable supplies of vitamin A, iron and riboflavin, as well as smaller amounts of other nutrients such as calcium, phosphorus and thiamine. Furthermore, they are one of the few foods that contain natural vitamin D and surprisingly the average egg yields only 77 calories.

Good fresh eggs are widely available in all our stores. The buyer may choose between grades AA, A and B, and sizes of extra large, large and medium. Grade and size, however, are not related; a large egg may be of the lowest quality and vice versa. Some persons select the grade according to their prospective use in cookery. The two top grades, for example, have rounder and thicker yolks and are preferable for poaching and frying.

The number of delectable dishes that depend on the egg is virtually endless. It is universally treasured and served in myriad ways, although the basic methods of cooking eggs by themselves is limited to baking, boiling, frying, poaching, scrambling and making into omelets. Eggs should always be cooked over low heat so the nutrients will not be destroyed.

These wonders of nature combine with just about every food we eat to make elegant and economic, vibrant and versatile creations which can be enjoyed from early morning to late evening. Eggs are also used to leaven cakes and souffles, clarify soups, coat breaded fish and poultry, thicken custards and sauces, emulsify salad dressings, bind together croquettes and meat loaves, and garnish salads and canapes.

Yogurt can be utilized simply in egg cookery. It gives, for example, extra lightness to such favorites as scrambled eggs and omelets. Yogurt is a perfect adornment for whole or sliced hard-cooked eggs and poached egg creations, and imparts flavor and goodness to souffles, casseroles and other baked dishes.

Cheese is also delicious, versatile and rich with essential food elements, a good source of protein, calcium and riboflavin. It is widely enjoyed by itself as a snack, appetizer or dessert, and is combined with other foods in all types of dishes.

There are over 400 types of natural cheeses and many processed varieties. They come in numerous styles, flavors and textures. American, Cheddar, cottage, cream, Parmesan and Swiss are kitchen staples. But we can buy both domestic and imported cheeses with names ranging from Asiago to Wensleydale.

All cheeses should be cooked over low heat, but some kinds cook better than others, such as American, Cheddar, Parmesan, Romano and Swiss. How much cheese is added to a dish depends on the type as sharper kinds will impart more flavor than milder varieties. Cheese, however, should never be overcooked as it becomes tough and stringy and its flavor changes.

Egg and cheese dishes made with yogurt are excellent for any occasion but especially for brunches, luncheons and suppers. They are easy to prepare, are elegant and economic, and are a boon to any cook searching for new ideas for nutritious and attractive dishes.

Oeufs sur le Plat Niçoise

This is a good company dish as the eggs are baked in the dish in which they will be served.

1 medium onion, minced	2 tablespoons olive or vege-
1 garlic clove, crushed	table oil

2 tablespoons tomato paste

½ teaspoon dried oregano

1½ cups plain yogurt

⅓ cup sliced olives (black, green or stuffed)

Salt, pepper to taste

6 thin slices cooked ham

6 thin slices Swiss cheese

6 eggs

Sauté the onion and garlic in the oil in a saucepan. Add the tomato paste and oregano and stir well. Mix in the yogurt, olives, salt and pepper. Cook over low heat for about 5 minutes to blend the flavors.

Arrange the ham slices in the bottom of an attractive shallow baking dish. Place a slice of cheese over each. Carefully break an egg onto each cheese slice and cover with the yogurt sauce. Bake in a preheated moderate (325°F.) oven for about 10 minutes, or until the eggs are set. Serve in the baking dish. Serves 6.

Bulgarian Green Beans and Eggs

The Bulgarians are very fond of vegetable-egg-yogurt creations such as this flavorful dish. It's an interesting variation of scrambled eggs and can be served for breakfast or luncheon.

1 medium onion, peeled and chopped

2 tablespoons butter or vegetable oil

1 tablespoon flour

Cayenne, salt, pepper to taste

1 cup chopped, cooked green beans

4 eggs, slightly beaten

1 cup plain yogurt

2 teaspoons chopped fresh dill

Sauté the onion in the butter until tender. Stir in the flour, cayenne, salt and pepper and cook about 1 minute. Add the green beans and mix well. Stir in the eggs, yogurt and dill and cook over low heat, stirring occasionally, until the ingredients are cooked. Serves 4.

Mushroom Egg Ragout from France

In French a *ragoût* is a stew, generally a well seasoned meat dish. But the term has been used also for any flavorful combination of ingredients such as this one. A good dish. to serve for an after the movie or theatre supper.

3 tablespoons butter or margarine	Freshly grated nutmeg, salt, pepper to taste
¼ cup minced green onions, with tops	6 hard-cooked eggs, shelled and chopped
1 pound fresh mushrooms, cleaned and sliced thinly	⅓ cup chopped fresh parsley
1 tablespoon flour	Paprika
1½ cups plain yogurt	3 English muffins, cut in halves and toasted

Melt the butter in a large saucepan. Add the onions and sauté until tender. Stir in the mushrooms and sauté for 4 minutes. Mix in the flour and cook several seconds. Gradually add the yogurt and then season with nutmeg, salt and pepper. Heat gently. Stir in the eggs and parsley and leave on the stove long enough to heat through. Serve on toasted English muffin halves garnished with paprika. Serves 6.

Turkish Eggs Poached in Yogurt

Yamurta çilbir, eggs with yogurt, is a typical luncheon dish in Turkey and could be served with a tomato-romaine salad and crusty white bread.

1 garlic clove, cut in half	1½ tablespoons vinegar
1 cup plain yogurt	3 tablespoons butter
Salt	2 teaspoons paprika
6 eggs	

Rub a bowl with the garlic and discard. Add the yogurt and a pinch of salt. Put the bowl in a warm place so the yogurt will become warm but not hot. Poach the eggs in water to which the vinegar has been added. Melt the butter and add the paprika. Serve the eggs with the yogurt spooned over them. Garnish with the butter and paprika. Serves 6.

Brunch Eggs on Tomato Slices

This is an attractive and easy-to-prepare dish which could be served for brunch. Crisp bacon or fried ham and warm whole wheat muffins would be excellent accompaniments.

1/3 cup minced green on-
    ions, with tops
1 medium garlic clove,
    crushed
4 tablespoons (about)
    vegetable oil
2 tablespoons tomato paste

1/2 teaspoon dried basil or
    marjoram
Salt, pepper to taste
2 cups plain yogurt
6 thick tomato slices
6 hot fried or poached eggs

Sauté the onions and garlic in 2 tablespoons of oil until tender. Stir in the tomato paste, basil, salt and pepper. Cook, stirring, for about 1 minute to blend the flavors. Add the yogurt and cook over low heat until the sauce is warm. Sauté the tomato slices in the remaining 2 tablespoons of oil, adding more if necessary. Serve each tomato slice topped with an egg and the yogurt sauce spooned over it. Serves 6.

Continental Anchovy Yogurt Eggs on Toast

Europeans are very fond of anchovy-flavored egg dishes which are served for breakfast or luncheon. This is a variation of an English favorite.

1 medium onion, peeled
    and chopped

2 tablespoons butter or
    margarine

8 to 10 anchovy fillets,
   minced
4 hard-cooked eggs, shelled
   and chopped

1½ cups plain yogurt
Black pepper to taste
Triangles of white toast

Sauté the onion in the butter in a skillet or saucepan until soft. Stir in the remaining ingredients, except the toast, and heat gently until the ingredients are hot and the flavors well mixed. Serve on toast points. Serves 4.

Company Cheese Sandwiches

Serve as a snack or light brunch or luncheon entrée.

6 slices white bread
6 thin slices Swiss cheese
6 eggs, fried and kept warm

¾ cup warm yogurt
Paprika

Cover each slice of bread with a slice of cheese and slide under the broiler until the cheese is bubbly and melted. Top each sandwich with a hot fried egg and 2 tablespoons of warm yogurt. Sprinkle with paprika. Serves 6.

Soybean Yogurt Eggs Orientale

Soybeans are inexpensive, rich in protein and do not contain any starch. They provide essential nutrients in many easy-to-prepare dishes such as this one.

½ cup minced green on-
   ions, with tops
⅓ cup diced green pepper
⅓ cup diced celery
1 cup chopped canned soy
   beans

1 to 2 teaspoons soy sauce
⅓ cup plain yogurt
6 eggs
Pepper to taste
2 tablespoons peanut or
   vegetable oil

Combine all the ingredients, except the oil, and mix well. Heat the oil in a medium-sized skillet and turn the egg mixture into it. Cook over low heat until almost set. Cut into quarters. Turn over and cook a little longer. Serves 4.

Armenian Eggs in Ground Beef with Yogurt

The Armenian cuisine is a rich and varied one that has many dishes known also in the neighboring Near Eastern countries. This is similar to one prepared also in Turkey.

1 medium onion, peeled and chopped	1/4 teaspoon allspice
1 garlic clove, crushed	Salt, pepper to taste
5 tablespoons butter or margarine	1/3 cup chopped fresh parsley
1/2 pound lean ground beef	4 eggs
3 tablespoons tomato paste	2 to 3 teaspoons paprika
	1 cup plain yogurt

Sauté the onion and garlic in 3 tablespoons of the butter in a skillet until tender. Add the ground beef and cook, separating with a fork, until the redness disappears. Stir in the tomato paste, allspice, salt and pepper. Add 1/2 cup of water and cook slowly, uncovered, about 15 minutes, or until the meat is tender. Stir in the parsley. With the back of a tablespoon make 4 depressions in the mixture. Break an egg into each depression. Mix the remaining 2 tablespoons of butter with the paprika. Mix with the yogurt and spoon over the eggs. Cook over a low fire, covered, until the eggs are set. Serves 4.

Smorgasbord Cheese Tomato Casserole

This is an appealing variation of a casserole called *ostlada* which is served traditionally with the hot buffet, or *smavarmt,* of the Swedish smorgasbord.

Butter or margarine
4 large tomatoes, peeled
    and sliced
4 hard-cooked eggs, shelled
    and sliced
Salt, pepper to taste

6 eggs
2 cups warm plain yogurt
½ teaspoon paprika
⅔ cup grated Swiss or
    Parmesan cheese

Butter a medium-sized casserole on all the inner surfaces, and arrange the tomato and egg slices in layers. Sprinkle with salt and pepper. Beat the eggs in a bowl to combine the whites and yolks. Add the yogurt and paprika and spoon over the casserole ingredients. Sprinkle the top with the cheese. Bake in a preheated hot (425°F.) oven for about 20 minutes, or until the mixture is set. Serves 4 to 6.

Piquant Creamed Eggs and Salmon on Whole Wheat Toast

A nourishing and interesting dish for luncheon or supper.

4 tablespoons butter or
    margarine
4 tablespoons flour
2 cups plain yogurt
1 teaspoon Worcestershire
    sauce
1 tablespoon drained
    capers
2 tablespoons ketchup

Salt, pepper, to taste
1 cup cleaned and flaked
    canned salmon
6 hard-cooked eggs, shelled
    and sliced
4 slices whole wheat bread,
    toasted
Paprika

Melt the butter in a large saucepan. Stir in the flour and cook 1 minute. Add the yogurt, Worcestershire, capers, ketchup, salt and pepper and cook over low heat for about 1 minute to blend the flavors. Stir in the salmon and eggs and leave on the stove until heated. Serve spooned over the toast and garnished with paprika. Serves 4.

Moroccan Scrambled Eggs

Moroccans, like other North Africans, are fond of well-seasoned dishes made with onions, garlic, tomatoes and red peppers. Yogurt combines well with and imparts a pleasing savor to these flavorful ingredients.

1 medium onion, chopped	1/4 teaspoon each of crushed
1 garlic clove, crushed	red pepper and dried
2 tablespoons butter or	oregano
margarine	Salt, pepper to taste
2 medium tomatoes, peeled	1/2 cup plain yogurt
and chopped	6 eggs, beaten
1 medium green pepper,	1/4 cup chopped fresh
cleaned and chopped	coriander or parsley

Sauté the onion and garlic in the butter in a skillet until tender. Add the tomatoes, green and red pepper, oregano, salt and pepper and cook slowly, covered, for about 10 minutes, or until the vegetables are cooked. Combine the yogurt, eggs and coriander in a bowl and then add to the vegetables. Mix gently and then cook over low heat, stirring now and then, until set. Serves 6.

Eggs Lorraine

There are a number of inviting culinary creations which are made with ham and cheese and named Lorraine for the lovely northeastern province of France. This is a variation of a famous egg dish and is a good brunch entrée.

6 slices thinly sliced	6 eggs
cooked ham	3/4 cup plain yogurt at
Butter	room temperature
6 thin slices Swiss cheese	Paprika

Arrange the ham slices in lightly buttered individual ramekins or small baking dishes. Cover each one with a slice of cheese and break an egg over each. Top each with 2 table-spoons of plain yogurt and sprinkle with paprika. Bake in a preheated hot oven (400°F.) for about 10 minutes, or until the eggs are set. Serves 6.

Mediterranean Luncheon Vegetables and Eggs with Yogurt

Such flavorful vegetables as eggplant, zucchini and to-matoes, great favorites in the Mediterranean countries, are combined with herbs and yogurt to make a colorful base for eggs.

1 medium onion, peeled and chopped

1 medium garlic clove, crushed

⅓ cup (about) olive or vegetable oil

1 small or ½ medium egg-plant, unpeeled and cubed

2 small zucchini, unpeeled and sliced

2 large tomatoes, peeled and chopped

½ teaspoon crumbled dried basil

½ teaspoon crumbled dried oregano or thyme

Salt, pepper to taste

1 cup plain yogurt

6 eggs

Chopped fresh dill

Sauté the onion and garlic in the oil in a skillet until soft. Add the eggplant cubes and zucchini slices, several at a time, and sauté until soft. Add more oil, if needed. Stir in the tomatoes, basil, oregano, salt and pepper and mix well. Cook slowly, over low heat, for 10 minutes. Stir in the yogurt and mix well. With the back of a spoon make 6 depressions in the mixture. Break an egg into each and cook, covered, over a low fire until the eggs are set. Garnish with dill. Serves 6.

Macedonian Poached Eggs in Spinach with Yogurt

The vast and picturesque province of Macedonia in southern Yugoslavia is noted for its unusual scenery and

medieval historical monuments. The cuisine is closely related to that of Greece and Turkey and yogurt is very popular fare. This is a typical luncheon dish.

*2 packages (10 ounces
    each) frozen chopped
    spinach, cooked and
    drained
Butter
8 eggs, poached and kept
    warm*

*2 garlic cloves, crushed
2½ cups plain yogurt
1 cup grated Parmesan
    cheese
3 tablespoons chopped
    fresh parsley*

Spoon the cooked and drained spinach into a buttered
shallow baking dish and with the back of a spoon make 8 depressions in it. Break 1 egg into each depression. Combine
the garlic, yogurt and grated cheese and spoon over the eggs.
Sprinkle with the parsley. Put under the broiler long enough
to become bubbly and golden on top. Serves 4 as an entrée.

Dieters' Cottage Cheese Yogurt Omelet

A low calorie creation which is attractive and delectable.
Serve for brunch or luncheon.

*6 eggs
1 cup creamed cottage
    cheese, beaten
½ cup plain yogurt
¼ cup minced green pep-
    per*

*¼ cup minced onion
¼ cup minced celery
2 tablespoons chopped
    fresh parsley
Salt, pepper to taste
3 tablespoons margarine*

Break the eggs into a large bowl and mix with a fork to
combine the whites and yolks. Add the remaining ingredients, except the margarine, and mix well. Melt the margarine in a medium skillet. Add the egg-cheese mixture and
tilt at once to spread evenly. Cook over low heat. Run a

knife or spatula around the edge of the pan and tilt the mixture so the liquid runs underneath. Continue cooking unti¹ the mixture is set and the surface is dry. Fold over and serve. Serves 4.

Omelette aux Fines Herbes

An interesting variation of a long-time French favorite which can be served for breakfast or as a light brunch or luncheon entrée.

6 eggs
6 tablespoons plain yogurt
3 tablespoons chopped chives
3 tablespoons chopped fresh parsley
¼ teaspoon each of crumbled dried basil and rosemary
3 tablespoons butter or margarine

In a large bowl beat the eggs with a fork or whisk until the yolks and whites are combined. Stir in the remaining ingredients, except the butter and mix well. Heat the butter in a medium-sized skillet and pour in the egg mixture. Cook over low heat. As it cooks run a knife or spatula around the edge and tilt the pan so the liquid runs under. When the mixture is set and the surface dry fold over and serve. Serves 2 or 3.

Mock Welsh Rabbit

A very popular cheese dish of Welsh origin, sometimes called rarebit as well as rabbit, is a good supper or late evening entrée. Yogurt imparts a particular appeal to this mock version of the traditional dish.

3 tablespoons butter or margarine
2 tablespoons flour
1½ cups plain yogurt
1 pound sharp Cheddar cheese, grated

½ teaspoon powdered
    mustard
1 teaspoon Worcestershire
    sauce

⅛ teaspoon cayenne or
    paprika
Salt, pepper to taste
Toast points

Melt the butter in a large saucepan. Stir in the flour and cook slowly, stirring, for about 1 minute. Add the remaining ingredients, except the toast points, and cook slowly, stirring, until the cheese melts and the mixture is creamy. Serve spooned over toast points. Serves 6.

Egg Yogurt Curry Indienne

A very interesting spice is turmeric, the root of a plant related to ginger. It is widely used in Indian cookery and imparts a bright gold color to dishes in which it is included. It also combines well with yogurt.

1 large onion, peeled and
    minced
2 tablespoons butter or
    margarine
2 teaspoons ground tur-
    meric
½ teaspoon chili powder
¼ teaspoon ground ginger

Salt, pepper to taste
1 teaspoon fresh lime or
    lemon juice
1 cup plain yogurt
6 hard-cooked eggs, shelled
    and cut into quarters
Chutney (optional)

Sauté the onion in the butter until soft. Add the turmeric, chili powder, ginger, salt and pepper and cook, stirring, about ½ minute. Add the lime or lemon juice, yogurt and eggs and leave on the stove long enough for the ingredients to heat through. Serve accompanied by chutney, if desired. Serves 4.

Souffle de Fromage

A long-time favorite, cheese souffle, can be served as a first course, entrée or accompaniment to other foods.

4 *eggs*	1 *cup grated Swiss or Gru-*
1 *additional egg white*	*yère cheese*
3 *tablespoons butter*	*Dash cayenne*
3 *tablespoons flour*	½ *teaspoon salt*
1 *cup plain yogurt at room*	⅛ *teaspoon pepper*
temperature	

Before starting to make the souffle, remove the eggs from the refrigerator to bring to room temperature. Separate, putting the yolks in a small bowl and the whites with the additional egg white in a larger bowl.

Melt the butter in a heavy saucepan and stir in the flour to form a *roux*. Cook, stirring, for 1 minute. Gradually add the yogurt and cook slowly, stirring, until thick and smooth. Add the cheese, cayenne, salt and pepper, and continue to cook slowly until the cheese is melted. Remove from the heat and cool a little. Beat the egg yolks until creamy and mix into the sauce. Beat the egg whites until stiff and carefully fold half of them into the cheese mixture. Then add the remaining half. Spoon into a buttered 1½ quart souffle dish or casserole. Bake, uncovered, in a preheated moderate oven (375°F.) for 30 to 35 minutes, until puffed up and golden. Serve at once. Serves 4.

Hawaiian Scrambled Eggs with Pineapple and Yogurt

An interesting variation of scrambled eggs which can be served as a main dish for luncheon or dinner.

3 *green onions, with tops,*	½ *cup plain or fruit-*
minced	*flavored yogurt*
2 *tablespoons peanut oil*	8 *eggs, beaten*
½ *cup diced green pepper*	*Salt, pepper to taste*
1 *cup drained pineapple*	
chunks	

Sauté the minced green onions in the oil in a large skillet until tender. Add the green pepper and sauté 1 minute. Combine the pineapple chunks, yogurt, eggs, salt and pepper in a bowl and pour into the skillet. Cook over low heat, stirring as for scrambled eggs, until the mixture is cooked. Serves 4 as a brunch or luncheon entrée.

Swiss Cheese Yogurt Quiche

Quiche, a pastry shell filled with an egg and cream custard combination is of French origin but has become an international favorite. Generally believed to have been first created in the region of Alsace-Lorraine and made simply with bacon, there are now many variations of *quiches* which include such ingredients as ham, crabmeat, salmon, cheese, onions, etc. Traditionally, a quiche is cooked in a fluted round metal pan with a removable bottom but it can be made also in a straight-sided cake pan or ordinary pie plate. Serve as a first course or light entrée for luncheon.

Pastry for 1 9-inch pie shell
1 cup grated Swiss cheese
3 large eggs
¾ cup evaporated milk

¾ cup plain yogurt at
  room temperature
Salt, freshly ground pepper
  and grated nutmeg to
  taste

Partially bake the pie shell and cool. Spread the cheese evenly over the surface. Break the eggs into a large bowl and mix with a fork or whisk to combine the yolks and whites. Add the remaining ingredients and continue to mix until they are well combined. Pour over the cheese. Bake in a preheated moderate (375°F.) oven for about 35 minutes, or until the custard is set and a knife inserted into it comes out clean. Remove from the oven and let stand a few minutes before cutting into wedges to serve. Serves 4 to 6.

Pasta, Rice and Other Grains

Edible seeds of the grass family, more commonly known as cereals or grains, have been man's most important food since the beginning of civilization. Unfortunately, the versatility of their gastronomic role is not well known or appreciated. There is an excellent repertoire of dishes made with barley, corn, millet, oats, rice, rye and wheat. Yogurt adds special appeal and goodness to them all.

Fruits of the field, as these foods are sometimes called, have been responsible for the foundations of all important civilizations. Those of the Middle East and Rome depended on wheat, barley and the millets. The ancient cultures of Asia were based on the growing of rice; whereas the early Central and South American civilizations relied primarily on the corn crop.

Cereals or grains have had such unparalleled prominence on the tables of mankind because they have been able to grow easily almost everywhere, yield an abundant crop, can be easily stored, and are inexpensive and nourishing.

Whole grains provide valuable nutrients, being rich in the B vitamins, protein, starch, iron and phosphorous. Therefore those which compose the entirety, or bran, germ and endosperm, are considered more healthy, but refined products also contain considerable goodness.

Cereals and grains are used extensively in our daily diet for every meal and in between as snacks. Wheat and rye, for example, are milled into flour which is essential to the making of breads and other baked goods and many of our everyday dishes. The hard durum wheat is important for the preparation of pasta products. Corn is processed into meal and grits, oil and syrup, as well as the popular corn flakes and many convenience foods.

Our stores have a wealth of grains in many varieties and forms. The buyer may select between a number of rices, pastas, oats, barleys and corn products. Health and specialty food stores and some super markets carry some lesser known but very appealing and nutritious grains which have long been appreciated in foreign countries, such as cracked wheat or *bulgur, cous cous,* buckwheat groats, millet and whole wheat.

Cooking pasta, rice and other grain dishes with the addition of yogurt provides the homemaker with many interesting everyday and company creations which have various roles in our menus. Some of this collection was created by inventive cooks many centuries ago. The innovative recipes add further good and inviting fare to the rewarding repertoire.

Polynesian Natural Brown Rice with Yogurt

Brown rice has an appealing nutty flavor and is very nutritious as during the milling process only the husks are removed and the essential food values are retained in part of the bran coat. It is particularly rich in B vitamins.

1 medium onion, peeled and minced

1 garlic clove, crushed (optional)

3 tablespoons peanut or vegetable oil

1 cup water

2 cups pineapple or orange juice

1 cup natural brown rice

½ teaspoon ground ginger

Salt, pepper to taste

1 cup pineapple or orange chunks

½ cup chopped nuts (pecans, walnuts or peanuts)

1 cup plain yogurt at room temperature

Sauté the onion and garlic in the oil in a large saucepan until tender. Add the water and juice and bring to a boil. Stir in the rice, ginger, salt, and pepper. Lower the heat and cook slowly, covered, for about 50 minutes, or until the grains are tender and the liquid is absorbed. Stir in the pineapple or orange chunks, nuts and yogurt and leave on the stove long enough to heat the ingredients. Serves 6.

Gourmet Green Noodles à la Creme

One of the best of our many pasta creations is the delicate spinach-flavored noodle generally called a green noodle. It is sold generally in packages and is a great company dish. Serve as an accompaniment to poultry or meat.

1/4 cup minced shallots or
    green onions
3 tablespoons butter
2 tablespoons flour
1 cup light cream
1 cup plain yogurt at room
    temperature

Salt, freshly ground pepper
    and grated nutmeg to
    taste
8 ounces medium green or
    spinach noodles,
    cooked and drained
Grated Parmesan cheese,
    preferably freshly
    grated

Sauté the shallots in the butter in a saucepan until tender. Stir in the flour and mix to form a *roux*. Gradually add the cream and then the yogurt, stirring as adding, and cook slowly until smooth and thickened. Season with salt, pepper and nutmeg. Toss in a large bowl with the cooked and drained green noodles and serve at once. Pass grated cheese with the dish. Serves 4.

Herbed Cracked Wheat Yogurt Casserole

A most appealing nutty flavored grain called cracked wheat or *bulgur* is commonly used in the cuisines of the Middle East. In America it is generally available in health stores or those specializing in Middle Eastern food products. It is well worth seeking.

2 tablespoons butter or
    margarine
1½ cups cracked wheat
    (bulgur)
3 cups chicken broth or 3
    chicken bouillon cubes
    and 3 cups water
1 medium onion, peeled
    and diced
1 medium green pepper,
    cleaned and diced

3 tablespoons vegetable oil
1 cup chopped fresh herbs
    (parsley, dill, basil, tar-
    ragon, and chives)
2 eggs
1 cup plain yogurt at room
    temperature
Salt, pepper to taste
Grated Parmesan cheese

Melt the butter in a medium-sized saucepan and add the cracked wheat. Sauté until golden. Pour in the chicken broth and bring to a boil. Lower the heat and cook slowly, covered, for about 25 minutes, or until most of the liquid is absorbed. Meanwhile, sauté the onion and green pepper in the oil in a small saucepan or skillet until tender. Remove from the heat and add to the cracked wheat. Stir in the remaining ingredients, except the cheese, and mix well. Spoon into a buttered baking dish and sprinkle the top generously with cheese. Bake in a preheated moderate oven (350°F.) for 30 minutes, or until done. Serves 6.

Yogurt Noodle Kugel from Israel

In Israel a baked pudding called a *kugel* is made in many variations and served as an accompaniment to other foods. This version would go well with poultry.

8 ounces broad noodles, cut
    into 2-inch pieces
1 cup cottage or pot cheese
2 eggs, separated
3 tablespoons melted
    butter
⅓ cup brown sugar

1 cup plain yogurt at room
    temperature
⅓ cup chopped golden
    raisins
⅓ cup chopped blanched
    almonds

Cook the noodles according to the package directions until just tender and drain. Turn into a large bowl. Add the cheese and mix well. Mix the egg yolks with a fork and add the butter and sugar. Stir into the noodle-cheese mixture. Add the yogurt, raisins and almonds and mix well. Beat the egg whites until stiff and fold into the mixture. Spoon into a buttered casserole or baking dish. Bake in a preheated moderate oven (350°F.) for about 30 minutes, or until the mixture is cooked. Serves 4 to 6.

Vegetarian Cous Cous with Yogurt

The traditional grain of North Africa is *cous cous,* made in the form of small dough pellets from hard durum semolina or millet and water. They are generally served with a stew-like topping of vegetables alone but meat or poultry may be included. Packaged *cous cous* is sold in American specialty food stores and some super markets. A special two part utensil with a perforated steamer top, designed for the cooking of *cous cous,* can also be purchased in specialty food stores.

1 package (500 grams, about 17 ounces) cous cous
½ cup water
2 large onions, peeled and sliced
¼ cup olive or vegetable oil
1 tablespoon crushed red pepper
½ teaspoon ground cumin
Salt, pepper to taste
1 can (1 pound 12 ounces)
tomatoes
3 medium zucchini, washed and sliced
2 small turnips, peeled and cubed
2 large green peppers, cleaned and cut into strips
1 can (1 pound, 4 ounces) chick-peas, drained
1½ cups plain yogurt
¼ cup chopped fresh coriander or parsley

Spread the *cous cous* over a tray and sprinkle with water.

Mix with the fingers. When ready to cook, put in a colander lined with cheese cloth or in the top of a *cous cous* steamer. Sauté the onions in the oil in a large kettle or the bottom of a *cous cous* steamer until soft. Add the pepper, cumin, salt and pepper and cook about 1 minute. Stir in the tomatoes and cook another minute. Add the zucchini, turnips and green peppers and a little water. Put the colander or steamer top with the *cous cous* over the vegetables. Cook, covered, about 30 minutes, or until the *cous cous* and vegetables are done. Stir the yogurt into the vegetables and add the coriander. To serve, spoon the *cous cous* onto a large platter and arrange the vegetables and liquid over and around it. Serves 6.

Note: Throughout the cooking check to see if more water should be added to the vegetables. There must be a fair amount of liquid because the *cous cous* cooking above the vegetables absorbs the liquid from them.

Caucasian Plov with Fruit and Yogurt

In Russia's picturesque southwestern province called the Caucasus a favorite rice dish called *plov* is made in interesting variations. Very often nuts and fresh or dried fruits are included. This is one good version.

1 cup dried apricots	*3 cups chicken broth*
½ cup seedless raisins	*1½ cups uncooked rice*
¼ teaspoon ground saffron	*Salt, pepper to taste*
(optional)	*1 cup plain yogurt at room*
3 tablespoons butter or	*temperature*
margarine	

Cover the apricots and raisins with boiling water and soak for 1 hour. Drain and cut the apricots into bite-size pieces. Steep the saffron in 2 tablespoons of hot water. Melt the butter in a saucepan. Add the chicken broth and bring to a boil. Mix in the rice and season with salt and pepper.

Add the apricots, raisins and saffron. Mix well. Lower the heat and cook slowly, covered, about 25 minutes, or until the rice is tender, the grains are separated and the liquid is absorbed. Stir in the yogurt and mix well. Serves 8.

Balkan Noodles with Yogurt Sauce

Serve this flavorful creation with pork or game.

1 package (8 ounces) egg noodles	3 tablespoons grated Parmesan cheese
1 large onion, peeled and chopped	Dash cayenne
	Salt, pepper to taste
2 garlic cloves, crushed	1 cup plain yogurt at room temperature
5 tablespoons butter or margarine	1 teaspoon paprika
3 tablespoons tomato paste	

Cook the noodles according to package directions and drain. Keep warm. Sauté the onion and garlic in 3 tablespoons of butter until tender. Stir in the tomato paste, cheese, cayenne, salt, pepper and yogurt. Mix well and heat gently. Remove from the heat and combine with the warm cooked noodles. Melt the remaining 2 tablespoons of butter and mix with the paprika. Spoon over the noodles and serve at once. Serves 6.

Yogurt Fried Rice

An Oriental favorite, fried rice, is enhanced with the addition of yogurt to the traditional ingredients.

⅓ cup chopped green onions, with tops	4 cups cold cooked rice
1 garlic clove, crushed	2 teaspoons minced fresh ginger (optional)
⅓ cup chopped cooked ham or pork	2 to 3 tablespoons soy sauce
	Pepper to taste
3 tablespoons peanut or vegetable oil	2 eggs, slightly beaten

½ to ¾ cup plain yogurt at   *Garnishes: slices of tomato,*
room temperature   *cucumber and green*
     onions

Sauté the onions, garlic and ham in the oil until tender. Stir in the rice, ginger, soy sauce and pepper and cook stirring, until the ingredients are warm. Combine the eggs and yogurt and add to the rice mixture. Cook, stirring, a little longer, until the eggs are cooked. Serve garnished with the tomatoes, cucumber and onions. Serves 4.

Barley and Mushrooms from Poland

Two favorite Polish foods, barley and mushrooms, are included in this nutritious and flavorful mixture which would be a good accompaniment for poultry or pork.

¼ cup butter or margarine   *2½ cups hot beef bouillon*
1 medium onion, peeled   *or consommé*
and chopped   *½ teaspoon dill seeds*
1 cup sliced fresh mush-   *Salt, pepper to taste*
rooms   *1 cup plain yogurt at room*
1 tablespoon fresh lemon   *temperature*
juice   *1 to 2 teaspoons paprika*
1 cup pearl barley

Melt the butter in a large heavy saucepan and sauté the onion in it until tender. Add the mushrooms and lemon juice and sauté 1 minute. Stir in the barley. Add the hot bouillon and dill seeds. Season with salt and pepper. Cook over low heat, tightly covered, about 1 hour or until the barley is tender and the liquid is absorbed. Stir in the yogurt and serve garnished with the paprika. Serves 6.

Indonesian Yellow Rice

In Southeast Asia yogurt and spices are combined with rice or noodles to make flavorful dishes which are served as accompaniments. This would be excellent with lamb.

1 *medium onion, peeled*
  and minced
1 *garlic clove, crushed*
3 *tablespoons peanut or*
  vegetable oil
1 *tablespoon turmeric pow-*
  der
1 *teaspoon ground ginger*

1 *teaspoon ground corian-*
  der
1 *cup uncooked rice*
1 *cup milk*
1 *cup plain yogurt at room*
  temperature
Salt, pepper to taste
Garnish: fried onion flakes

Sauté the onion and garlic in the oil until tender. Stir in the turmeric, ginger and coriander and cook several seconds. Add the rice and sauté about 2 minutes. Pour in the milk and yogurt. Season with salt and pepper. Cook slowly, covered, for about 25 minutes, or until the grains are tender. Serve garnished with the fried onion flakes made by frying chopped onions in butter until golden. Serves 4.

Ukrainian Buckwheat Casserole

The most popular "cereal" dish of Russia is *Kasha,* prepared generally with buckwheat groats. When cooked, the nourishing, flavorful and inexpensive groats are eaten generally as a porridge or combined with other ingredients and baked.

1 *cup buckwheat groats*
2 *cups milk, scalded*
⅓ *cup small curd cottage*
  cheese

½ *cup plain yogurt*
2 *eggs, beaten*
Salt to taste

Cook the buckwheat groats in a skillet without fat, stirring, until the grains are golden and roasted. Mix with the scalded milk, cottage cheese, yogurt, beaten eggs, salt and pepper. Spoon into a buttered baking dish. Cook, tightly covered, in a preheated moderate oven (350°F.) about 40 minutes, or until cooked. Serve with melted butter, if desired. Serves 8.

Vermicelli with Curried Yogurt Sauce

An interesting accompaniment for grilled hamburgers to serve outdoors or inside.

2 tablespoons butter or
    margarine
2 medium onions, peeled
    and sliced
1 or 2 garlic cloves, crushed
2 to 3 teaspoons curry
    powder

1 tablespoon flour
Salt, pepper to taste
2 cups plain yogurt at
    room temperature
8 ounces vermicelli, cooked
    and drained

Heat the butter in a medium sized saucepan and add the onions and garlic. Sauté until tender. Stir in the curry powder and cook 1 minute. Add the flour, salt and pepper and cook, stirring, about 1 minute. Add the yogurt and leave on the stove long enough to heat. Serve the drained, cooked vermicelli with the yogurt sauce. Serves 4.

Armenian Cracked Wheat Pilaf with Yogurt

Another very good and flavorful dish made with cracked wheat, called also *bulgur*.

3 tablespoons butter or
    margarine
1 medium onion, peeled
    and chopped
2 medium tomatoes, peeled
    and chopped
1 cup medium cracked
    wheat (bulgur)

$2\frac{1}{2}$ to 3 cups beef bouillon
    or consommé
Salt, pepper to taste
1 cup plain yogurt
2 teaspoons chopped fresh
    dill

Melt the butter in a skillet and sauté the onion in it until tender. Add the tomatoes and cook slowly about 1 minute, or until mushy. Stir in the cracked wheat and sauté, stirring constantly, until golden. Add the bouillon, the salt and pepper and mix well. Bring to a boil. Lower the heat and cook slowly, covered, about 40 minutes, or until the cracked wheat is tender and the liquid is absorbed. Heat the yogurt gently and spoon over the cracked wheat. Garnish with the dill. Serves 4.

Yogurt Spaghettini à la Español

A Spanish-flavored yogurt sauce attractively adorns the very popular spaghettini in this interesting dish. Serve as a light entrée or as an accompaniment to meatballs.

1 large onion, peeled and minced	1 cup tomato sauce
1 or 2 garlic cloves, crushed	½ teaspoon cayenne
1 cup diced smoked ham	Salt, pepper to taste
3 tablespoons olive or vegetable oil	1 cup plain yogurt at room temperature
2 medium tomatoes, peeled and chopped	⅓ cup chopped fresh parsley
	8 ounces spaghettini

Sauté the onion, garlic and ham in the oil in a medium saucepan or skillet until the onion is soft. Add the tomatoes and cook slowly about 1 minute. Stir in the tomato sauce, cayenne, salt and pepper and cook slowly, uncovered, for 10 minutes. Stir in the yogurt and parsley and cook slowly another 5 minutes. While the sauce is cooking, cook the spaghettini according to the package directions until just tender. Drain and serve at once covered or mixed with the sauce. Serves 4.

German Bread Dumplings with Dilled Yogurt

The Germans are great devotees of dumplings which they prepare in fascinating variety and consume in great quantity. Among them are *semmelklösse* or bread dumplings.

3 cups stale white bread
    cubes, ½ inch each
½ cup milk
3 slices bacon, chopped
1 small onion, peeled and
    minced
2 eggs, beaten

2 tablespoons chopped
    fresh parsley
1¾ cups (about) sifted all-
    purpose flour
2 cups plain yogurt
2 tablespoons chopped
    fresh dill
Salt, pepper to taste

Place the bread cubes in a large bowl and cover with the milk. Fry the bacon and pour off all of the fat except 1 tablespoon. Add the onion and sauté in the fat until tender. Add the cooked bacon, sautéed onion, eggs and parsley to the bread cubes and mix well. Stir in the flour, enough to make a stiff dough, and beat well. With floured hands shape the dough into six balls. Drop into a large kettle of boiling salted water. Boil, uncovered, until the dumplings rise to the top. Cover and cook 10 to 15 minutes, or until done. Test by tearing one apart with two forks. Remove with a slotted spoon and drain. While cooking, heat gently the yogurt, dill, salt and pepper and serve spooned over the dumplings. Serves 6.

Grecian Lenten Rice and Chick Peas with Yogurt

Grecian cooks have created many nourishing and flavorful dishes for their stringent lenten season. One, made traditionally with rice and chick peas, is further enriched with yogurt.

1 large onion, peeled and
    minced
1 to 2 garlic cloves,
    crushed
¼ cup olive or vegetable
    oil

2 medium tomatoes, peeled
    and chopped, or 2
    tablespoons tomato
    paste
2 cups water

1 cup uncooked long grain
    rice
½ teaspoon dried oregano
Salt, pepper to taste
1 can (1 pound, 4 ounces)
    chick-peas, drained

1 cup plain yogurt at room
    temperature
⅓ cup chopped fresh pars-
    ley
2 tablespoons butter, mar-
    garine or oil

Sauté the onion and garlic in the oil in a large saucepan until tender. Add the tomatoes or tomato paste and cook about 1 minute. Add the water and bring to a boil. Mix in the rice, oregano, salt and pepper and lower the heat. Cook slowly, covered, for about 20 minutes, or until the grains are tender and the liquid is absorbed. Stir in the chick-peas and yogurt and leave on the stove long enough to heat the ingredients. Mix in the parsley and butter just before serving. Serves 6.

Yogurt Macaroni and Cheese

One of our oldest and most familiar pasta creations is macaroni and cheese but it takes on a particular glamour when additional ingredients are included.

2 cups macaroni elbows
4 thin slices bacon, diced
1 medium onion, peeled
    and diced
1 cup canned tomatoes
    with liquid
½ teaspoon dried basil

Salt, pepper to taste
1 cup plain yogurt at room
    temperature
1 cup diced Cheddar or
    American cheese
Grated Parmesan cheese
Butter or margarine

Cook the macaroni according to the package directions until just tender and drain. Cook the bacon in a small skillet until almost crisp and drain off all except 3 tablespoons of the fat. Add the onion and sauté until tender. Add the tomatoes, basil, salt and pepper and cook slowly, uncovered, for 5 minutes to blend the flavors. In a large bowl combine the tomato sauce, yogurt, Cheddar or American cheese and cooked and drained macaroni. Spoon into a buttered round or a shallow baking dish. Sprinkle the top generously with grated Parmesan and dot with butter. Bake in a preheated moderate oven (350°F.) for about 25 minutes, or until the mixture is hot and bubbly. Serves 4.

Coconut Rice from Thailand

The fruit of a palm called coconut is one of the most important foods in Southeastern Asia. Both the white meat and the milk are widely used in all of the inviting cuisines. Use either the fresh or packaged kind in this recipe.

2 medium onions, peeled and minced	½ teaspoon ground cloves
3 to 4 tablespoons peanut or vegetable oil	½ teaspoon ground coriander
4 cups cooked long grain white rice	½ teaspoon ground cinnamon
2 teaspoons grated fresh ginger or 1 teaspoon ground ginger	2 cups plain yogurt at room temperature
	1 to 1½ cups flaked coconut

Sauté the onions in the oil in a large skillet until tender. Mix in the remaining ingredients and cook slowly, covered, for 10 minutes. Serves 4.

Central European Noodle Cottage Cheese Casserole

An interesting luncheon entrée or accompaniment for meat, poultry or fish.

¼ pound thinly sliced bacon	1¼ cups plain yogurt
1 package (8 ounces) wide noodles, cooked and drained	1 cup cottage cheese
	⅓ cup minced onion
	Salt, pepper to taste

Cook the bacon until crisp. Drain, reserving 3 tablespoons of fat, and crumble. Set aside. Mix the reserved fat with the cooked noodles, yogurt, cottage cheese and onion. Season with salt and pepper. Spoon into a buttered medium casserole. Sprinkle the top with the crumbled bacon. Bake in a preheated moderate oven (350°F.) for about 30 minutes, or until done and the top is golden. Serves 8.

Near Eastern Tomato Pilaf with Yogurt

In the Near Eastern cuisines there are countless variations of a rice dish called generally *pilaf* but one of the most commonly enjoyed is this simple creation.

4 tablespoons butter or margarine	1 cup long grain rice
2 tablespoons tomato paste or 1 large tomato, peeled and chopped	Salt, pepper to taste
	½ cup plain yogurt at room temperature
2 cups chicken broth	1 tablespoon chopped fresh dill

Heat 2 tablespoons of the butter in a saucepan. Add the tomato paste or tomato and cook about 1 minute for the paste and 2 or 3 minutes for the tomato. Add the broth and bring to a boil. Stir in the rice and season with salt and pepper. Lower the heat and cook slowly, covered, about 20 minutes, or until the liquid is absorbed and the grains are tender. Stir in the remaining 2 tablespoons of butter, the yogurt and dill and mix well. Serves 4.

Oriental Noodles with Yogurt

Serve with skewered beef or pork cubes.

¼ cup peanut or vegetable oil	½ cup shredded raw chicken or pork

2 medium onions, peeled
   and sliced
1 medium green pepper,
   cleaned and cut into
   strips
3 water chestnuts, sliced
   thinly

1 tablespoon toasted sesame
   seeds (optional)
1 to 2 tablespoons soy sauce
Pepper to taste
1 cup plain yogurt at room
   temperature
8 ounces thin noodles,
   cooked and drained

Heat the oil in a skillet or saucepan. Add the chicken or pork and sauté until cooked. Add the onions and green peppers and sauté 1 minute. Stir in the water chestnuts, sesame seeds, soy sauce and pepper and cook 1 minute. Stir in the yogurt and noodles and leave on the stove long enough to heat through. Serves 4.

Buffet Tomato Yogurt Spaghetti

A colorful and tasty baked spaghetti dish which could be served as an accompaniment to cold meats or poultry or, if desired, as an entree.

2 medium onions, peeled
   and minced
2 garlic cloves, crushed
¼ cup olive or vegetable
   oil
¼ cup tomato paste
1 teaspoon crumbled dried
   oregano
Grated Parmesan cheese

½ teaspoon crumbled
   dried rosemary
2 cans (1 pound each) to-
   matoes, undrained
Salt, pepper to taste
1 cup plain yogurt at room
   temperature
1 pound thin spaghetti,
   cooked and drained

Sauté the onions and garlic in the oil in a saucepan or skillet until tender. Stir in the tomato paste, oregano and rosemary and mix well. Add the tomatoes and break them up into small pieces. Season with salt and pepper. Cook slowly, uncovered, for 15 minutes. Remove from the heat and stir in the yogurt. Spoon half of the sauce in a large shallow baking dish. Cover with the cooked and drained spaghetti and spread the remaining sauce over it. Sprinkle the top generously with cheese. Bake in a preheated moderate oven (350°F.) for 15 minutes, or until hot and bubbly. Serves 8 as an entrée or 10 to 12 as an accompaniment.

Indian Lentil and Rice Khichiri

This is a very inexpensive and nourishing dish which is eaten as staple fare in India. Generally made with a number of spices it can also be flavored with curry powder as a substitute. Serve as a vegetarian entrée or accompaniment to such meats as lamb, beef or poultry.

1 medium onion, peeled and chopped	*Salt, pepper to taste*
1 garlic clove, crushed	*4-5 cups water*
2 tablespoons butter or margarine	*1 cup uncooked long grain rice*
1 teaspoon turmeric powder	*1 cup dried lentils*
¼ teaspoon ground cloves	*1 cup plain yogurt at room temperature*
½ teaspoon ground cinnamon	*Garnishes: Sliced hard-cooked eggs, crisply fried onion rings*
1 teaspoon ground cardamom	

Sauté the onion and garlic in the butter in a large saucepan until tender. Stir in the spices and salt and cook 1 minute. Add 4 cups of water and bring to a boil. Mix in the rice and lentils and lower the heat. Cook slowly, covered, for about 30 minutes, or until the rice and lentils are tender and the liquid is absorbed. Add more water while cooking, if needed. Stir in the yogurt and remove from the heat. Serve garnished with the eggs and onion rings, if desired. Serves 8 to 10.

Seafood

Among our great gastronomic treasures none is more delightful and fascinating than seafood. Fortunately we have an abundant and wide variety of foods from oceans, seas, streams and lakes. Fresh, frozen, canned or cured, the bountiful harvest enriches our cookery. Yogurt marries well with both fish and shellfish.

The world's marine treasure trove has long been important to the survival of man. Over the centuries we could not have existed without these nutritionally rich denizens of the sea. Few foods contain high quality proteins, minerals and vitamins in such proportions. Seafood is valued for its iron, iodine, and vitamins A and D, among other assets.

Such is the plethora of edible fish and shellfish of all descriptions and qualities which is caught at all times of the year in the waters of the world that the exact number is probably unknown. In America the average person generally cooks and enjoys a very few kinds of seafood. Yet more than 240 species are sold in our stores and markets. It is unfortunate that we are not better acquainted with more of them as seafood is not only rich in nutritive value, but is comparatively inexpensive and can provide a welcome change of pace in our menus. Low-fat diets can include many varieties of lean fish and shellfish which, pound for pound, contain only half to two-thirds the calories of beef or pork.

Fresh fish is always a particular treat and, either whole or cut into steaks, fillets or chunks, is available throughout the year, although the kind may vary according to the season and region. In selecting fish it is important to choose the freshest, which should have bright, clear and bulging eyes; red and slime-free gills; firm flesh; and bright colored scales. Shellfish, such as clams, crabs, lobsters, oysters, scallops, and shrimp, are gourmet delicacies which are more expensive than fish and should also be carefully purchased.

Our packaged frozen seafood has increased in such quantity and quality during the past several years that the homemaker has a world of great products with which to produce elegant and-healthful dishes. Labels on the myriad canned products should be carefully studied so the buyer will completely understand the weight and the nature of the contents.

Seafood can be cooked in a variety of ways—baked, broiled, fried, grilled, poached or steamed. Because it is naturally tender it should be cooked only at low or medium temperatures and for a short period. Cooking at high temperatures and for a long time destroys the flavor and nutritive value. Generally it should be served right after cooking.

Yogurt is one of the many flavorings, such as butter, wine, herbs, mushrooms, onions and other vegetables, which enhance seafood dishes. Cooking and serving these creations will enhance one's interest in these delectable denizens of the deep and reward the diner with unusual and delicious fare.

Caucasian Fish Stuffed with Buckwheat Groats

In the Caucasus of southern Russia this dish is traditionally made with bream, a freshwater fish closely related to the sunfish. In this country the bluegill is sometimes called a bream. Any small white-fleshed fish may be used as a substitute.

2 medium onions, peeled and chopped

6 tablespoons butter or margarine

2 cups cooked buckwheat groats

2 hard-cooked eggs, shelled and chopped

2 tablespoons chopped fresh parsley

2 tablespoons chopped fresh dill

Salt, pepper to taste

4 1-pound white-fleshed fish (porgies, crappies, sunfish), cleaned

Fine dry bread crumbs

1 cup plain yogurt at room temperature

Sauté the onions in 3 tablespoons of butter. Add the cooked buckwheat groats, chopped eggs, parsley, dill, salt and pepper. Mix well. Wash the fish and wipe dry. Sprinkle the cavities with salt and fill with the stuffing. Arrange in a buttered shallow baking dish. Melt the remaining 3 tablespoons of butter and sprinkle over the fish. Sprinkle also with bread crumbs. Bake in a preheated hot oven (400°F.) about 10 minutes, or until the fish are almost tender. Spoon the yogurt over the fish and cook another 5 minutes. Serves 4.

Fish Potato Stew with Yogurt from Albania

The small rugged country of Albania which faces the Adriatic Sea has many robust fish stews which are generally made with whatever ingredients are on hand. This is typical of them.

2 large onions, peeled and sliced

2 garlic cloves, crushed

3 tablespoons olive or vegetable oil

3 tablespoons tomato paste

2 cups fish broth or water

1 cup dry white wine

6 potatoes, peeled and sliced thickly

1/4 teaspoon dried basil

1 bay leaf

Salt, pepper, cayenne to taste

2 pounds white-fleshed fish, cleaned and cut up

1 cup plain yogurt at room temperature

3 tablespoons chopped fresh parsley

Sauté the onions and garlic in the oil in a large saucepan or kettle until tender. Stir in the tomato paste and mix well. Add the fish broth, wine, potatoes, basil, bay leaf, salt, pepper and cayenne. Cook over a medium flame, covered, for 10 minutes. Add the fish and cook slowly about 15 minutes, or until the potatoes and fish are tender. Remove and discard the bay leaf. Mix in the yogurt and parsley and serve with crusty white bread, if desired. Serves 4 to 6.

Shrimp Yogurt Croquettes

We have inherited many fine croquette recipes from France where the name originated. It derives from the verb *croquer*, to crunch. The French hold these deep-fried creations in high esteem and serve them as elegant entrées, preferably piled in a mound on a linen napkin.

3 tablespoons butter or
    margarine
¼ cup flour
½ cup light cream
½ cup plain yogurt or
    1 cup yogurt
Salt, pepper, freshly grated
    nutmeg to taste

2 eggs
2 cups chopped, cleaned,
    cooked shrimp
2 tablespoons chopped
    fresh parsley
Juice of 1 lemon
Fine dry bread crumbs
Fat for deep frying

Melt the butter in a saucepan. Stir in the flour and cook 1 minute to form a *roux*. Gradually add the cream and yogurt and cook slowly, stirring, until the sauce is smooth and thick. Season with salt, pepper and nutmeg. Separate 1 egg. Beat the yolk with a fork and mix some of the hot sauce with it. Return to the saucepan. Add the shrimp, parsley and lemon juice. Mix well and take off the stove. Beat the egg white until stiff and fold carefully into the mixture. Spoon into a flat dish, spreading evenly, and cool. Divide the mixture into 12 equal parts. Form each into a 2-inch ball. Chill for 1 hour. Beat the remaining egg lightly. Roll each croquette in bread crumbs, then in beaten egg, and again in bread crumbs. Refrigerate for 1 hour. Fry in hot deep fat (300° on a frying thermometer) until golden. Drain. Serve with yogurt, if desired. Serves 4 to 6.

French Seafood Coquille

A *coquille* in French is a shell, but the name has been given also to a dish made in that shape and the preparation put in it. Coquilles are marvelous for entertaining as they can be prepared beforehand, are delectable, and can be served as first courses or light entrées.

1 pound small shrimp in the shell	1 cup plain yogurt at room temperature
1 pound white-fleshed fish fillets (sole, flounder, cod, halibut, haddock)	½ teaspoon crumbled dried rosemary or thyme
3 tablespoons minced shallots or green onions	1 tablespoon fresh lemon juice
¼ cup butter or margarine	Salt, pepper to taste
¼ cup flour	Fine dry bread crumbs
1 cup light cream	Grated Parmesan cheese

Shell and clean the shrimp. Cook the fillets in a little water until just fork tender. Drain and cut into ½ inch pieces. Sauté the shallots in the butter in a medium saucepan. Add the shrimp and sauté until they turn pink, just a few minutes. Stir in the flour and cook 1 minute. Gradually add the cream and yogurt and cook slowly, stirring, until thickened. Add the rosemary, lemon juice, salt, pepper and pieces of white fish. Cook another 5 minutes. Remove from the stove and spoon into 6 large coquilles or individual ramekins. Sprinkle the top of each with bread crumbs and cheese and dot with butter. Bake in a preheated hot oven (400°F.) about 10 minutes, or until bubbly and the tops are golden. Serves 6.

Light Luncheon Shellfish Fruit Salad

Serve with warm wholewheat rolls or dainty sandwiches.

3 cups cooked cleaned shrimp, lobster or crab meat	1 cup chopped celery
	2 cups drained pineapple chunks or diced grapefruit sections
1 cup diced green peppers	

¾ to 1 cup plain yogurt
1 tablespoon fresh lemon
    juice

Salt, pepper to taste
Lettuce leaves
Slivers of blanched almonds

Combine the first four ingredients in a bowl. Mix together the yogurt, lemon juice, salt and pepper and add to the shrimp mixture. Serve on lettuce leaves garnished with almonds. Serves 6.

Herbed Baked Fish Steaks

Fresh herbs add attractiveness, flavor and goodness to this easy-to-prepare luncheon or dinner entrée.

2 pounds fish steaks (cod,
    haddock, halibut, fresh
    tuna, salmon, sword-
    fish)
Salt, pepper to taste
1 cup plain yogurt at room
    temperature
Juice of 1 lemon

2 tablespoons minced green
    onions
1 cup soft bread crumbs
2 tablespoons melted
    butter
½ cup chopped fresh herbs
    (parsley, dill, basil)

Sprinkle the steaks on both sides with salt and pepper and place in a shallow baking dish. Combine the yogurt, lemon and onions and spoon over the steaks. Mix the bread crumbs, butter and herbs and sprinkle over the yogurt mixture. Bake in a preheated moderate oven (350°F.) for about 25 minutes, or until the fish is easily flaked with a fork. Serves 4 to 6.

Truites à la Crème from Grenoble

A specialty of the fine restaurants of Grenoble, a captivating city in the French Alps, is fresh brook trout. This is an adaptation of a typical recipe.

6 medium brook trout,
    fresh or frozen and
    defrosted
Salt, pepper
Milk
Flour

5 tablespoons butter
1 cup plain yogurt at room
    temperature
1 cup blanched slivered
    almonds

Wash the trout and dry thoroughly. Sprinkle inside and out with salt and pepper. Dip each one in milk and then in flour and sauté in 4 tablespoons of melted butter in a large skillet until golden brown on both sides. Add more butter, if needed. Place the trout on a hot plate and keep warm. Add 1 tablespoon of butter to the drippings and stir in 1 tablespoon of flour. Mix well. Add the yogurt and heat gently, stirring. Season with salt and pepper. Spoon over the trout and garnish with the almonds previously browned in butter. Serves 6.

Maryland Crab Meat Artichoke Casserole

Maryland is famous for its many creations made with blue crabs taken from the Chesapeake Bay. Crab meat and artichokes with a yogurt sauce make a succulent company casserole.

2 tablespoons minced green
    onions
½ cup butter or margarine
½ cup flour
Dash cayenne
Salt, pepper to taste
1½ cups milk
1½ cups plain yogurt at
    room temperature

1 cup cleaned and flaked
    claw crab meat
1½ cups cut-up cooked
    artichoke hearts
½ cup buttered bread
    crumbs
Grated Parmesan cheese

Sauté the onions in the butter in a saucepan until tender. Stir in the flour and mix well. Cook 1 minute. Season with cayenne, salt and pepper. Gradually add the milk and yogurt and cook slowly, stirring, until thickened and smooth. Mix in the crab meat, artichoke hearts and bread crumbs. Spoon into a buttered casserole. Sprinkle the top with grated Parmesan. Bake in a preheated moderate oven (350°F.) for 30 minutes. Serves 4 to 6.

Note: This dish may be prepared also with canned or frozen crab meat.

Bengali Yogurt Fish

Bengal in East India has a diet based primarily on fish which is eaten for all meals. Traditional dishes such as this one are richly flavored with spices and yogurt. Serve with rice or lentils.

1 pound white-fleshed fish (sole, flounder, cod, haddock, halibut)
1 cup plain yogurt at room temperature
½ teaspoon turmeric powder
2 teaspoons minced fresh ginger
½ teaspoon chili powder

2 tablespoons butter or margarine
1 garlic clove, crushed
1 large onion, peeled and chopped
½ teaspoon each ground cloves, cardamom and cinnamon
1 teaspoon sugar

Cut the fish into 4 portions. Put in a shallow dish and cover with the yogurt, turmeric, ginger and chili. Mix well and leave to marinate 1 hour. Heat the butter in a skillet. Add the garlic and onion and sauté until tender. Stir in the spices and sugar. Cook 1 minute. Add the fish and yogurt mixture and cook slowly, covered, for 5 minutes or until tender. Serves 4.

Nourishing Salmon Yogurt Loaf

Devotees of natural foods will enjoy this rewarding loaf as it includes a number of their favorites which are combined to make an inviting luncheon or dinner entrée.

2 cups diced wholewheat
    bread
1/4 cup soybean or corn oil
1/4 cup wheat germ
2 cans (1 pound each)
    pink or red salmon,
    cleaned, drained and
    flaked
1 cup plain yogurt

3 large eggs, slightly beaten
4 teaspoons fresh lemon
    juice
1/4 cup chopped onion
1/4 cup minced fresh pars-
    ley
1 teaspoon sage (optional)
Salt, pepper to taste

Combine all the ingredients in a large bowl and mix
well. Pack into a buttered loaf pan. Bake in a preheated
moderate oven (350°F.) about 35 minutes, or until cooked.
Unmold on a platter and garnish with sliced stuffed olives,
if desired. Serves 8.

Newfoundland Creamed Cod and Eggs with Capers

Much of our supply of cod comes from the Grand Bank
of Newfoundland and the cooks of Canada's Atlantic island
use this nourishing fish in many everyday dishes. This one is
a good supper entrée to serve with boiled or mashed potatoes.

2 tablespoons minced
    onion
1/4 cup butter or margarine
1/4 cup flour
Cayenne, salt, pepper to
    taste

1 cup milk
1 cup plain yogurt
2 cups flaked uncooked cod
1/3 cup drained capers
4 hard-cooked eggs

Sauté the onion in the butter until tender. Mix in the
flour to form a roux. Season with cayenne, salt and pepper.
Gradually add the milk and yogurt and cook slowly, stirring,
until thickened. Add the cod and capers and continue to
cook slowly for about 12 minutes, or until the fish is tender.

Stir occasionally. While cooking chop the egg whites and sieve the egg yolks. Add the whites to the cod mixture and serve garnished with the yolks. Serves 4.

Turkish Pilaf Stuffed Mackerel

The Turkish cuisine is rich with imaginative fish preparations as they have a plethora of seafood from nearby waters. This is one of the best and most attractive.

1 mackerel, 3½ to 4
   pounds, dressed
Salt
1 cup minced onions
⅓ cup olive or vegetable
   oil
¼ cup pine nuts
½ cup uncooked long-
   grain rice
1 cup chicken broth or
   water

½ teaspoon ground cinna-
   mon or nutmeg
Pepper to taste
¼ cup currants or raisins,
   previously soaked in
   warm water and
   drained
½ cup chopped fresh pars-
   ley
1 cup plain yogurt at room
   temperature
1 lemon, sliced thinly

Wash and dry the mackerel. Sprinkle inside and out with salt. Set aside. Sauté the onions in 2 tablespoons of the oil in a saucepan until tender. Add the pine nuts and rice and sauté until the rice is translucent. Add the chicken broth, cinnamon, salt and pepper and bring to a boil. Lower the heat and cook slowly, uncovered, about 20 minutes, until the grains are tender and the liquid is absorbed. Add the currants and ⅓ cup of parsley and mix well. Remove from the heat. Stuff the fish with the rice mixture and close the opening with skewers or sew with thread. Place the fish in a buttered shallow baking dish. Cover with the remaining oil, parsley, yogurt and lemon slices. Bake in a preheated moderate oven (350°F.) about 1 hour, or until the fish flakes easily when tested with a fork. While baking, baste occasionally with the drippings. Serves 6.

Chafing Dish Lobster Elegante

This elegant lobster-yogurt dish may be prepared in a chafing dish at the table or in a saucepan on the stove. Excellent for a supper or late-evening party.

2 packages (9 ounces each) frozen lobster tails
2 tablespoons butter or margarine
1/4 cup minced green pepper
1 1/2 tablespoons flour
Salt, pepper to taste
1 cup milk
1 egg, beaten

1/2 cup plain yogurt at room temperature
1 can (2 ounces) sliced mushrooms, drained
1/2 teaspoon prepared mustard
1/4 cup grated Parmesan cheese
Buttered toast

Cook the lobster tails according to package directions and then cut into 1/2 inch pieces. Melt the butter in a chafing dish or medium saucepan and sauté the green pepper in it for 2 minutes. Add the flour, salt and pepper and mix well. Gradually add the milk, stirring as adding, and cook about 2 minutes. Spoon some of the hot mixture into a small bowl and mix with the egg. Return to the dish. Cook 1 minute. Stir in the yogurt, and then the lobster, mushrooms, mustard and cheese. Leave over the heat long enough to heat through. Serve over buttered toast. Serves 4 to 6.

Hungarian Fish Pörkölt

Hungarians prepare flavorful fish stews called *pörkölt*, a kind of goulash which is flavored with onions and paprika. Sour cream is used in the traditional recipe but yogurt is a good substitute.

3 medium onions, peeled and sliced

1/4 cup bacon drippings or shortening

2 to 3 tablespoons paprika
3 large tomatoes, peeled
    and chopped
3 medium green peppers,
    cleaned and chopped
Salt, pepper to taste

3 pounds white-fleshed
    fish, cleaned and cut
    into large pieces
1 cup plain yogurt at room
    temperature

Sauté the onions in the drippings in a large saucepan or kettle until tender. Add the paprika and cook 1 minute. Stir in the tomatoes and green peppers and cook about 5 minutes, or until soft. Season with salt and pepper. Push aside and add the fish pieces. Spoon the vegetables over them and add just a little water. Cook slowly, covered, about 25 minutes, or until fork tender, adding a little more water, if needed. Stir in the yogurt and remove from the heat. Serves 6.

Slavic Baked Fish

A typical fish dish prepared in the Slavic regions of Eastern Europe is flavored traditionally with sour cream but it can be prepared also with yogurt.

2 pounds fish (halibut,
    cod, haddock, mack-
    erel), cleaned
Flour
Salt, pepper to taste
¼ cup butter or margarine
2 hard-cooked eggs, shelled
    and sliced

1 cup sliced fresh mush-
    rooms
1 tablespoon paprika
½ cup grated Parmesan
    cheese
1 cup plain yogurt at room
    temperature
Fine dry bread crumbs

Leave the fish whole or cut into large pieces. Dust with flour and sprinkle with salt and pepper. Melt the butter and spoon into a shallow baking dish. Place the fish in the dish. Cover with the hard-cooked egg and mushroom slices. Sprinkle with paprika. Combine the cheese and yogurt and spoon evenly over the other ingredients. Sprinkle with bread crumbs. Bake in a preheated moderate oven (350°F.) for about 25 minutes, or until the fish flakes easily with a fork. Serves 6 to 8.

Grilled Jumbo Shrimp in Yogurt Marinade

A gourmet delicacy for an outdoor meal.

2 pounds raw jumbo
    shrimp
1 or 2 garlic cloves, crushed
1 tablespoon fresh lemon
    juice

1 cup plain yogurt
1/4 teaspoon tabasco
Freshly ground pepper to
    taste

Split each shrimp shell down to the tail being careful not to cut the meat. Put in a bowl and cover with the remaining ingredients. Leave to marinate for 1 to 2 hours. Turn over now and then. Put the shrimp on small skewers and cook over a charcoal fire for 10 to 15 minutes, turning once. Baste with the marinade. Serves 4 to 6.

Supper Salmon Yogurt Souffle

A delicate and delicious creation to serve at an early or late evening supper. Offer an attractive salad and warm dark rolls with it.

3 tablespoons butter or
    margarine
3 tablespoons flour
Dash nutmeg
Salt, pepper to taste
1 cup plain yogurt at room
    temperature

3 eggs, separated
1 can (1 pound) red or
    pink salmon, drained,
    cleaned and flaked
1/2 teaspoon crumbled
    dried rosemary

Heat the butter in a saucepan and stir in the flour. Season with nutmeg, salt and pepper. Slowly add the yogurt and cook slowly, stirring, until the mixture thickens. Stir a little of the hot mixture into the beaten egg yolks and return to the saucepan. Add the salmon and rosemary. Beat the egg whites until stiff and fold carefully into the salmon mixture. Spoon into a buttered casserole or souffle dish. Bake in a preheated moderate oven (350°F.) for about 45 minutes, or until done. Serve at once. Serves 6.

Shrimp Curry from India

This is a good dish for a buffet. Serve with rice and a salad.

¼ cup butter, margarine or vegetable oil	1 tablespoon ground coriander
2 large onions, peeled and chopped	Salt, pepper to taste
2 garlic cloves, crushed	3 pounds raw shrimp, shelled and deveined
1 tablespoon turmeric powder	4 medium tomatoes, peeled and chopped
2 teaspoons chili powder	2 cups plain yogurt at room temperature
1½ teaspoons ground cumin	

Heat the butter in an extra-large skillet and add the onions and garlic. Sauté until soft. Stir in the turmeric and chili powders, cumin, coriander, salt and pepper and cook over low heat, stirring, for 1 minute. Add the raw shrimp and cook, stirring about, until just pink. Add the tomatoes and cook slowly, covered, for 10 minutes. Stir in the yogurt and cook another 5 minutes. Serves 12.

Note: The dish can be prepared with curry powder instead of the spices, if desired.

Filets De Sole à la Florentine

A type of cookery called *à la* Florentine refers generally to eggs, fish or poultry served on a bed of spinach and topped with a cheese-flavored cream sauce. The name derives from the lovely art center of Florence in Italy.

5 tablespoons butter or margarine

2 tablespoons minced onion (optional)

2 packages (10 ounces each) frozen chopped spinach, partially thawed

Dash freshly grated nutmeg

Salt, pepper to taste

1½ pounds fresh or thawed frozen sole or flounder fillets

1½ cups water

4 tablespoons flour

1 cup light cream or milk

1 cup plain yogurt at room temperature

1 cup shredded Swiss, American or Gruyère cheese

Fine dry bread crumbs

Melt 2 tablespoons of butter in a large saucepan and add the onion. Sauté until tender. Add the spinach and cook slowly, covered, until just tender. Season with nutmeg, salt and pepper and spoon into a buttered shallow baking dish. Spread evenly. Put the fillets and water in a large skillet and cook slowly, covered, until just tender, about 7 minutes. Remove the fillets with a slotted spoon and arrange over the spinach. Melt the remaining 3 tablespoons of butter in a saucepan and add the flour to form a *roux*. Gradually add the cream and then the yogurt and cook slowly, stirring, until thickened and smooth. Add the cheese and cook over low heat, stirring occasionally, until melted. Season with salt and pepper. Spoon over the fish. Sprinkle the top with bread crumbs and dot with butter. Bake in a preheated moderate oven (350°F.) for 20 minutes, or until hot and bubbly. Serves 4 to 6.

Scalloped Clams with Yogurt

Clams are rich with protein and contain fair amounts of calcium and iron. They are also low in calories. This dish is a good one to serve weight-watchers.

1 can (about 7½ ounces)
    minced clams
¼ cup butter or margarine
1 small onion, peeled and
    minced
3 tablespoons flour
1 cup plain yogurt at room
    temperature
½ cup clam liquid

½ teaspoon dry mustard
¼ teaspoon celery salt
Cayenne, salt, pepper to
    taste
2 hard-cooked eggs, shelled
    and chopped
Fine dry bread crumbs
Grated Parmesan cheese

Drain the clams, reserving the liquid. Melt the butter in a saucepan and sauté the onion in it. Mix in the flour and add the yogurt and clam liquid. Cook slowly, stirring, until thickened. Add the mustard, celery salt, cayenne, salt, pepper and eggs. Spoon into a buttered shallow baking dish and sprinkle with bread crumbs and cheese. Bake in a preheated moderate oven (350°F.) for about 25 minutes, or until hot and bubbly. Serves 4.

Serbian Baked Fish with Yogurt

The Serbians of Yugoslavia enjoy a combination of Balkan and Hungarian inspired dishes and are fond of heavily spiced foods and yogurt. Serve with rice or potatoes and crusty dark bread.

1 whole fish (sea bass, cod,
    mackerel), about 3
    pounds, cleaned
3 large onions, peeled and
    sliced
2 or 3 garlic cloves, crushed
⅓ cup olive or vegetable
    oil
1 to 2 tablespoons paprika
3 tablespoons tomato paste

½ teaspoon oregano or
    thyme
3 tablespoons chopped
    fresh parsley
Salt, pepper to taste
1½ cups dry white wine or
    water
2 tablespoons flour
1 cup plain yogurt at room
    temperature

Arrange the fish in a buttered baking dish. Sauté the onions and garlic in the hot oil until tender. Add the paprika and cook 1 minute. Stir in the tomato paste, oregano, parsley, salt, pepper and wine. Pour over the fish and bake in a preheated hot oven (400°F.), allowing about 10 minutes per pound, until tender, basting occasionally with the pan juices. Remove the fish to a hot platter and keep warm. Stir the flour into the pan juices. Add the yogurt and mix well. Cover over low heat, stirring, until thickened. Serve with the fish. Serves 4 to 6.

Poached Halibut Steaks with Mushroom Yogurt Sauce

Halibut is one of our finest and most important salt water fish and is taken from both the northern Atlantic and Pacific oceans. Its firm and flavorful white flesh is appreciated throughout the country. Halibut is particularly desirable in the form of steaks.

2 pounds halibut steaks
2 cups water
1 onion slice
1 lemon slice
2 or 3 parsley sprigs
1 bay leaf
4 peppercorns, bruised
Salt
1 can (4 ounces) sliced mushrooms, drained

1/4 cup butter or margarine
1 tablespoon fresh lemon juice
2 tablespoons flour
Freshly ground pepper and grated nutmeg
1 cup plain yogurt at room temperature

Put the halibut steaks in a large skillet and cover with the water, onion, lemon, parsley, bay leaf, peppercorns and 1½ teaspoons salt. Simmer gently, covered, about 12 minutes, or until the fish is fork tender. Remove the steaks to a platter and keep warm. Strain the liquid and reserve.

Sauté the mushrooms in the butter and lemon juice in

a saucepan for 3 minutes. Stir in the flour and cook 1 minute. Season with salt, pepper and nutmeg. Stir in 1 cup of the reserved fish broth and cook slowly, stirring. Add the yogurt and leave on the stove until heated. Pour over the halibut steaks and garnish with chopped dill or parsley, if desired. Serves 4 to 6.

Greek Island Fish Plaki

A popular way of preparing fish in the lovely Greek Islands is by baking it on a bed of vegetables which may vary according to the season. Yogurt provides additional appeal and savor to this type of cooking which in Greece is called *plaki*.

1 4-pound whole fish, dressed, or 3 pounds fish fillets (bass, halibut, bluefish, mackerel)
Salt, pepper to taste
2 medium onions, peeled and sliced
3 medium leeks, white parts only, cleaned and sliced
2 garlic cloves, crushed
⅓ to ½ cup olive or vegetable oil
4 large tomatoes, peeled and sliced
2 bay leaves
1 teaspoon dried oregano or thyme
1½ cups plain yogurt at room temperature
2 medium lemons, sliced
⅓ cup chopped fresh parsley

Wash the fish and wipe dry. Sprinkle inside and out with salt and pepper. Sauté the onions, leeks and garlic in the olive oil in a skillet until tender. Add the tomatoes, bay leaves, oregano and season with salt and pepper. Sauté 10 minutes. Spoon into a shallow baking dish and spread evenly. Arrange the fish over the mixture. Pour the yogurt over the fish. Place the lemon slices over it and sprinkle with the parsley. Bake in a preheated moderate oven (350°F.) about 30 minutes, or until the flesh flakes easily with a fork. The

time will be longer for the whole fish than for the fillets.
Serves 4 to 6.

Tempting Tuna Yogurt Mousse

The word mousse derives from the French for foam or
froth and is used for light hot or cold savory or sweet dishes
which can be served as first courses or entrées for luncheon
or supper. This is an easy to prepare and inexpensive version.

2 cans (6½ or 7 ounces)
    tuna, drained and
    flaked
1 tablespoon grated onion
2 teaspoons fresh lemon
    juice
2 teaspoons Worcestershire
    sauce
¼ teaspoon dried basil or
    oregano

1 cup plain yogurt
Salt, pepper to taste
4 egg whites
2 tablespoons butter or
    margarine
2 tablespoons flour
1 cup milk or plain yogurt
Dash cayenne
4 egg yolks

Break up the tuna as fine as possible in a bowl. Add the
next five ingredients and mix well. Season with salt and pepper. Beat the egg whites until stiff and fold into a greased 1½
quart baking dish. Cook in a preheated moderate oven
(350°F.) for about 45 minutes, or until the ingredients are
cooked.
While the mousse is cooking prepare the sauce by first
melting the butter in a saucepan. Stir in the flour. Add the
milk or yogurt and cook slowly, stirring, until smooth and
thickened. Season with cayenne, salt and pepper. Mix the
eggs with a fork in a small bowl. Stir in some of the hot sauce
and then return to the pan. Serve the hot mousse with the
sauce. Serves 6.

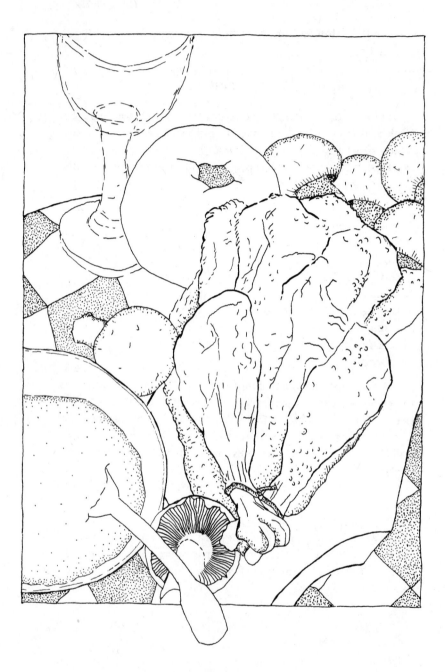

Poultry

The great variety of poultry products are accorded places of honor on our dining tables and treasured for everyday and company meals. Any of our domesticated fowl such as chickens, turkeys, ducklings, geese and Rock Cornish hens are prepared as enticing entrées and are also used in many other dishes. Yogurt combines with all of them to provide a rewarding repertoire of versatile and easy to prepare creations.

Fanciers of poultry are wise in frequently selecting any of the readily available kinds, either fresh, frozen or canned, for cookery. They are inexpensive, moderate in calories, and provide such essential nutrients as iron, thiamine, niacin and riboflavin.

Once poultry was considered as luxury fare and served primarily for Sunday, holiday or company meals. In recent years modern production, processing and shipping methods have provided the average homemaker with such a wide variety in readily available supply that poultry has become one of our most widely used foods. Stringent laws assure us of superb products at all times of the year.

Poultry can be baked, barbecued, braised, broiled, fried, roasted, stewed or combined with other foods to make innumerable intriguing dishes. The type of cookery will often depend on the age of the particular fowl. Broiler-fryers, for example, are very young chickens and thus are more suitable for barbecuing, braising, frying and broiling. Tom turkeys which are older and much larger are preferably roasted.

Of the various poultry products chicken is by far the most popular and widely used. Native to Southeast Asia it has traversed the world and become relished in all cuisines. Yogurt was probably first combined with chicken in India as a marinade to tenderize the bird and impart additional flavor to it. This is still the custom and is one well worth adopting in our own cookery.

Yogurt is an excellent ingredient to add to chicken or other poultry dishes which are cooked slowly on top of the stove. Throughout Southeast Asia, from India to the South Seas, there are a wide number of spicy creations commonly called curries which rely on the marriage of poultry and yogurt sauces. In our own country we have many creamed specialties which can feature these two foods. Our cookery also features superb baked or roasted dishes which are simple to prepare and fun to serve.

Poultry specialties, made either with chicken, turkey, duckling, geese or Rock Cornish hens and including yogurt, offer culinary delights which will please the family and happily surprise guests, for the choice ranges from the ordinary supper scalloped turkey and peas to the exotic Indian chicken *tandoori*.

Hungarian Paprika Chicken

This is one of the many flavorful paprika dishes which the Hungarians created. It is made traditionally with sour cream.

6 tablespoons lard or
    shortening
3 large onions, peeled and
    sliced
1 or 2 garlic cloves, crushed
1 to 2 tablespoons paprika
2 frying chickens, about
    2½ pounds each,
    cut up
Salt, pepper to taste

1½ cups chicken broth or
    1½ cups water and 1½
    chicken bouillon cubes
3 large tomatoes, peeled
    and sliced
2 large green peppers,
    cleaned and sliced
1 tablespoon flour
2 cups plain yogurt at room
    temperature

Heat the lard or shortening in a large skillet. Add the onions and garlic and sauté until tender. Mix in the paprika and cook 1 minute. Add the chicken pieces and cook on both sides until golden. Season with salt and pepper. Add the chicken broth and cook very slowly, covered, for 20 minutes. Add the tomatoes and green peppers and cook another 10 minutes, or until the chicken is tender. Mix the flour with the yogurt and stir into the chicken mixture. Leave on the stove long enough to heat through. Serve with noodles or dumplings. Serves 6.

French Supremes de Volaille avec Yaourt

A glorious French creation is a boneless raw breast of chicken called a *supreme de volaille* which is cooked very briefly and served in a rich cream sauce.

4 half chicken breasts	*1½ cups sliced fresh mush-*
Salt, white pepper to taste	*rooms*
¼ cup fresh lemon juice	*¼ cup chicken broth*
¼ cup butter or margarine	*¼ cup dry white wine*
1 small onion, peeled and	*2 teaspoons flour*
minced	*1 cup plain yogurt at room*
	temperature

Remove the skin from each chicken breast. Loosen the flesh from the bone of each. Pull out the pieces of cartilage. Cut the meat away from the bones. Pull out the white tendons. Sprinkle the chicken with salt, pepper and 1 tablespoon of lemon juice. Melt the butter in a skillet and sauté the chicken in it for 6 to 8 minutes, until white or, if pressed with the finger, it is soft but springy. Do not overcook. Remove from the heat and keep warm. Add the onion and mushrooms to the drippings and sauté for 4 minutes. Season with salt and pepper. Add the broth and wine and cook over high heat until syrupy. Combine the flour and yogurt and stir in. Cook slowly until the mixture thickens slightly. Season with salt, pepper and add the remaining lemon juice. Pour over the chicken and serve. Serves 4.

Siamese Chicken Curry

Curry is one of Thailand's (or Siam's) favorite dishes and the housewives make a special spice mixture or paste for each kind. This is a variation of the traditional dish.

1 teaspoon ground cori-
    ander
½ teaspoon chili powder
2 teaspoons turmeric pow-
    der
½ teaspoon cayenne
1 to 2 tablespoons anchovy
    paste
2 tablespoons wine vinegar
Salt, pepper to taste

2 frying chickens, about
    2½ pounds each, cut
    up
½ cup peanut or vegetable
    oil
2 medium onions, peeled
    and chopped
2 garlic cloves, crushed
1¼ cups (about) chicken
    broth
1 cup plain yogurt at room
    temperature

Combine the coriander, chili, turmeric, cayenne, anchovy paste, vinegar, salt and pepper to make a paste. Wash the chickens and wipe dry. Brown in the oil on both sides in a large skillet. Remove or push aside and add the onions and garlic to the drippings. Sauté until tender. Mix in the spicy paste. Return the chicken to the skillet and add the chicken broth. Cook slowly, covered, for 20 minutes, adding more broth if needed. Add the yogurt and continue to cook slowly, about 10 minutes longer, or until tender. Serves 8.

Spitted Chicken with Plum Sauce, Russian Style

This is a favorite dish in southern Russia where outdoor cookery is very popular.

2 broiler chickens, about
    2½ pounds each

Salt, pepper to taste
1 cup butter or margarine

1½ cups puréed cooked
   plums
1½ cups plain yogurt

1 garlic clove, crushed
2 tablespoons chopped
   fresh dill

Wash the chickens and wipe dry. Season inside and out with salt and pepper. Arrange on a skewer exactly in the center. Secure the legs and wings to the spit with strong thread. Brush well with butter. Cook about 1 hour, or until tender, brushing occasionally with butter. Remove from the spit. Serve with the plum sauce (recipe below). Serves 8.

Plum Sauce

Combine the puréed plums, yogurt, garlic and dill and season with salt and pepper. Heat gently until hot. Add a little water if a thinner sauce is desired.

Brunch Creamed Chicken with Mushrooms

A good dish for a weekend or holiday brunch. Double the recipe for a buffet meal.

4 tablespoons butter or
   margarine
1 cup sliced fresh mush-
   rooms
1 tablespoon fresh lemon
   juice
Dash grated nutmeg
4 tablespoons flour
1 cup light cream

1 cup plain yogurt at room
   temperature
2 cups diced cooked white
   chicken
Salt, pepper to taste
2 tablespoons dry sherry
   (optional)
Toast points
Paprika

Melt the butter in a large saucepan and add the mushrooms and lemon juice. Sauté 3 minutes. Season with nutmeg and stir in the flour. Gradually add the cream and yogurt and cook slowly, stirring, until thickened. Add the chicken, salt and pepper and cook over low heat until the ingredients are warm. Stir in the sherry, and spoon over warm toast points. Garnish with paprika. Serves 6.

Yugoslavian Roast Goose in Yogurt Sauce

In Yugoslavia, and neighboring countries as well, the goose is esteemed fare, particularly for holidays. This is one variation.

2 *medium onions, peeled and sliced*
3 *tablespoons bacon drippings or shortening*
1 *bay leaf, crumbled*
1 *lemon, sliced*
Salt to taste

10 *peppercorns, bruised*
1 *small young goose, about 5 pounds, cut up*
1 *tablespoon flour*
2 *cups plain yogurt at room temperature*

Sauté the onions in the bacon drippings or shortening until tender. Add the bay leaf, lemon slices, salt, peppercorns and 1 cup of water. Bring just to a boil. Pour into a roasting pan. Rub the goose pieces with salt and prick the skin in several places. Arrange over the onion mixture. Roast in a preheated slow oven (325°F.) about 3 hours, or until tender. Spoon off any accumulated fat. While cooking, turn the pieces over a few times. When cooked, remove the goose to a platter. Discard the bay leaf and peppercorns and add the flour and yogurt to the pan drippings. Mix well and heat through. Strain and pour over the goose. Serves 6 to 8.

Breast of Chicken Parisienne

An appealing entrée for a company luncheon or dinner which can be essentially prepared beforehand and reheated. Add the yogurt shortly before serving.

2 *whole chicken breasts, cut into halves*

Salt, pepper to taste
⅓ *cup butter or margarine*

¼ cup minced chives or
    green onions
½ pound fresh mush-
    rooms, cleaned and
    sliced
1 tablespoon fresh lemon
    juice

½ cup dry white wine
½ teaspoon crumbled
    dried rosemary
Salt, pepper to taste
1 cup plain yogurt at room
    temperature
1 tablespoon flour
Watercress

Wash the chicken breasts and wipe dry. Season with salt
and pepper. Melt the butter in a skillet and sauté the chicken
breasts on both sides until tender. Remove with a slotted
spoon to a plate. Add the chives, mushrooms and lemon juice
to the drippings and sauté 3 minutes. Return the chicken to
the skillet and stir in the wine, rosemary, salt and pepper
and cook slowly, covered, about 20 minutes, or until tender.
Combine the yogurt and flour and stir into the chicken. Cook
slowly, covered, another 5 minutes. Serve garnished with
watercress. Serves 4.

German Hasenpfeffer with Yogurt

A well known German marinated rabbit creation called
hasenpfeffer means literally hare pepper and is made traditionally with sour cream. Frozen rabbit is available generally
in supermarkets.

2 fresh or frozen rabbits
    (2½ to 3 pounds
    each), cut into serving
    pieces
Equal parts of wine vinegar
    and water to cover the
    rabbit pieces
2 medium onions, peeled
    and sliced
2 medium bay leaves
4 juniper berries

4 whole cloves
2 tablespoons sugar
6 peppercorns, bruised
Salt
Flour
Pepper
⅓ cup (about) butter or
    margarine
½ cup plain yogurt at
    room temperature

THE YOGURT COOKBOOK

Put the rabbit pieces in a large crock or kettle and add the vinegar, water, onions, bay leaves, juniper berries, cloves, sugar, peppercorns and salt. Let stand, covered, in a cool place for 2 days. Turn over the rabbit pieces 1 or 2 times daily. When the marinating is finished, take out the rabbit and strain the marinade, reserving it. Wipe the rabbit dry and dust with flour, seasoned with salt and pepper. Fry in butter or margarine until golden on all sides. Add some of the strained marinade and cook very slowly, covered, until the rabbit is tender, about 1 hour. Add more marinade as needed while cooking. Mix in the yogurt and remove from the stove. Serves 6 to 8.

Chicken with Parsley and Yogurt from Denmark

The Danes are very fond of a traditional chicken dish which is flavored simply with parsley, butter and cream. Yogurt imparts further appeal to it.

1 roasting chicken (about 4 pounds)	1 large bunch parsley with stems removed
Salt, pepper	1 cup plain yogurt at room temperature
1/2 cup butter	2 tablespoons flour

Wash the chicken and pat dry. Sprinkle on the inside and out with salt and pepper. Put 1/4 cup of butter and the parsley in the cavity of the chicken. Melt 1/4 cup of butter in a large casserole or kettle and add the chicken. Braise on all sides over moderate heat until golden, turning carefully with 2 large wooden spoons so the skin will not be pierced. Pour in a little water and cook slowly, covered, for 45 minutes to 1 hour, until tender, turning over once while cooking. When done, remove the chicken to a warm platter and keep warm. Add the yogurt to the juices, and after scraping up the drippings, quickly bring to a boil. Mix the flour with a little water and stir into the yogurt. Cook over medium heat, stirring, until smooth. Season with salt and pepper. Take the parsley from the chicken cavity and serve it with the chicken. Serve the gravy separately in a gravy boat or bowl. Serves 4 to 6.

Javanese Braised Spicy Chicken

On the enchanting Indonesian island of Java favorite chicken dishes are richly flavored with a medley of spices. Serve this interesting one with rice or noodles.

1 frying chicken, about 3½ pounds, cut up	2 teaspoons ground coriander
¼ cup peanut or vegetable oil	½ teaspoon chili powder
1 large onion, peeled and sliced	Dash ground ginger
1 garlic clove, crushed	Salt, pepper to taste
1 teaspoon ground turmeric	1 tablespoon flour
	1 tablespoon fresh lime or lemon juice
	1 cup plain yogurt at room temperature

Wash the chicken and wipe dry. Brown the chicken on both sides in the oil in a skillet. With tongs remove to a plate. Add the onion and garlic to the drippings and sauté until tender. Stir in the turmeric, coriander, chili powder, ginger, salt and pepper and cook 1 minute. Return the chicken to the skillet. Combine the flour, lime juice and yogurt and add to the chicken. Cook slowly, covered, for 30 minutes. Serves 4.

Smorgasbord Chicken Salad from Sweden

A delectable cold chicken creation which can be served as a part of a smorgasbord or buffet or as a light luncheon entrée.

3 cups diced cooked cold
    white meat of chicken
½ cup mayonnaise
½ cup plain yogurt
1 tablespoon curry powder

Salt, pepper to taste
Garnishes: wedges of hard-
    cooked eggs, capers,
    olive slices, finely
    chopped dill pickle

Combine the chicken with the mayonnaise, yogurt and curry powder. Season with salt and pepper. Spoon onto lettuce leaves on a platter and serve decorated with the garnishes. Serves 6.

Indian Chicken Tandoori

In northern India this yogurt marinated chicken is generally barbecued on an outdoor grill.

2 broiler fryers, about 2½
    pounds each
1½ cups plain yogurt at
    room temperature
1½ tablespoons lime or
    lemon juice
1½ tablespoons melted
    butter or margarine

1 or 2 garlic cloves, crushed
1 teaspoon chili powder
2 whole cardamoms, re-
    moved from pods and
    crushed
½ teaspoon ground cori-
    ander
¼ teaspoon ground ginger

Split the chickens in half. Remove and discard the backbones. Remove all the skin except that on the wings. Make tiny slits in several places in the flesh. Combine the remaining ingredients. Place the chicken in a large shallow baking dish or bowl and cover with the yogurt mixture. Marinate at least 6 hours or overnight. Turn about several times. When ready to cook arrange the chicken on a broiler rack and brush with the marinade. Broil as far away as possible from the heat about 50 minutes, turning once, or until tender. Serves 4.

Note: The chicken may be cooked also on an outdoor grill over medium coals.

Poulet Vallee d'Auge

This recipe derives from France's picturesque northwestern region of Normandy and is named for the Valley of Auge, the heart of the great cider and Calvados (apple brandy) country. It is rich and elegant.

6 single chicken breasts
Salt, pepper to taste
⅓ cup butter
⅓ cup Calvados or apple-jack
2 tablespoons finely chopped shallots or green onions

½ teaspoon crumbled dried thyme
2 tablespoons chopped fresh parsley
½ cup chicken broth
2 egg yolks
1 cup plain yogurt at room temperature

Wash the chicken breasts and pat dry. Season with salt and pepper. Brown on both sides in the butter in a heavy skillet. Add the Calvados and ignite it with a match. When the flames subside add the shallots, thyme and parsley and mix well. Add the broth and cook slowly, covered, about 25 minutes, or until the chicken is just tender, adding more broth or Calvados while cooking, if needed. Remove the chicken to a warm platter and keep warm. Scrape the drippings and bring the juices to a boil. Combine the egg yolks and yogurt in a bowl and stir with a whisk until smooth. Pour in some of the hot juices and mix well. Return to the skillet and cook over low heat, stirring, until the sauce begins to thicken. Correct the seasoning. Spoon over the chicken. Serve garnished with parsley. Serves 6.

Broiled Chicken with Yogurt Tomato Sauce

Cook and serve either outdoors or inside. Offer a cold rice salad or baked noodle casserole, a green salad and hot crusty rolls with the chicken.

3 tablespoons vegetable oil
1 tablespoon wine or cider
   vinegar
2 teaspoons dark brown
   sugar
2 teaspoons Worcestershire
   sauce

1 tablespoon grated onion
3 tablespoons tomato paste
Salt, pepper to taste
1 cup plain yogurt at room
   temperature
4 half broiling chickens

Combine the first six ingredients in a saucepan. Season with salt and pepper and bring to a boil. Cook briskly 1-2 minutes to blend the flavors. Remove from the heat and stir in the yogurt. Arrange the chicken in a shallow baking dish and cover with the yogurt sauce. Leave to marinate 3 to 4 hours. Cook the chicken over a medium fire, skin side down, until browned on one side and turn over. Baste with the sauce while cooking. Cook about 30 minutes, or until tender. Or broil in a preheated broiler about 20 minutes on each side, basting with the sauce while cooking. Serves 4.

Southern Fried Chicken in Yogurt Gravy

A long-time American favorite takes on further appeal when made with a yogurt-flavored gravy.

2 frying chickens, about 3
   pounds each, cut up
Flour
Salt, pepper to taste
½ cup (about) shortening
   or vegetable oil
1 medium onion, peeled
   and sliced

1 cup diced green pepper
   or celery
6 tablespoons flour
1½ cups milk
1½ cups yogurt at room
   temperature
¼ teaspoon poultry sea-
   soning
¼ teaspoon sage

Wash the chicken and wipe dry. Dredge with flour seasoned with salt and pepper. Heat the shortening in a large skillet and fry the chicken on both sides until golden. With tongs remove to a casserole or shallow baking dish. Add the onion and pepper to the drippings and sauté until tender. Stir in the flour and slowly add the milk and yogurt. Mix in the poultry seasoning and sage and pour over the chicken. Bake in a preheated moderate oven (325°F.) for 1 hour or until the chicken is tender. Serves 8.

Baked Yogurt Chicken from Rumania

This baked chicken is flavored with such popular Rumanian foods as paprika, mushrooms, dill and yogurt.

1 frying chicken, 2½ to 3 pounds, cut up
Salt, pepper to taste
6 tablespoons butter or margarine
2 tablespoons flour
1 tablespoon paprika
2 cups yogurt at room temperature

¼ pound fresh mushrooms, cleaned and sliced
2 tablespoons fresh lemon juice
2 tablespoons chopped fresh dill or parsley

Wash the chicken pieces and wipe dry. Sprinkle with salt and pepper. Melt 4 tablespoons of butter in a large skillet and fry the chicken pieces in it until golden on all sides. With tongs remove to a buttered shallow baking dish. Sprinkle the flour and paprika into the pan juices and cook, stirring, for 1 minute. Stir in the yogurt and mix well. Spoon over the chicken pieces. Sauté the mushrooms in the remaining 2 tablespoons of butter and the lemon juice for 1 minute and spoon over the casserole ingredients. Sprinkle with the dill. Bake, covered, in a preheated moderate oven (325°F.) for about 1¼ hours, or until the chicken is tender. Serves 4.

Pakistan Chicken Korma

A favorite chicken dish from Pakistan called *Korma* is a type of curry made with yogurt and spices.

8 chicken thighs or other
    small pieces
2 medium onions, peeled
    and chopped
1 garlic clove, crushed
2 cups plain yogurt at room
    temperature
Salt, pepper
1 tablespoon butter or mar-
    garine

1 teaspoon grated fresh
    ginger
1 teaspoon turmeric pow-
    der
½ teaspoon ground cumin
⅓ cup tomato purée
Garnishes: chopped cucum-
    ber, green onions and
    parsley

Place the chicken thighs in a shallow baking dish or bowl and cover with 1 chopped onion, the garlic and yogurt, and season with salt and pepper. Leave to marinate for 6 hours or overnight. Cook in a skillet over medium heat, uncovered, about 20 minutes or until most of the yogurt has evaporated.

Sauté the remaining onion in the butter and add the remaining ingredients, except the garnishes. Spoon into the skillet and add a little water. Continue to cook slowly, covered, until the chicken is tender, 15 minutes or longer. Add a little water if the chicken sticks to the pan. Serve topped with the garnishes. Serves 4.

Supper Scalloped Turkey and Peas

A nourishing easy to prepare supper dish which can be made with leftover cooked turkey.

¼ cup minced green
    onions, with tops
¾ cup diced green pepper
3 tablespoons (about)
    butter
1 cup cooked green peas
1 cup turkey or beef gravy
¾ cup diced celery

2 cups chopped cooked
    turkey
½ cup plain yogurt at
    room temperature
1 tablespoon parsley flakes
Fine dry breads
Grated Parmesan cheese
Salt, pepper to taste

Sauté the onions, celery and green pepper in 2 tablespoons of butter until tender. Mix with the peas, gravy, turkey, yogurt, and parsley. Season with salt and pepper and spoon into a shallow baking dish. Sprinkle the top with the bread crumbs and cheese and dot with butter. Bake in a preheated moderate oven (350°F.) for about 25 minutes, or until the ingredients are bubbly and the top is golden. Serves 4 to 6.

Long Island Orange Yogurt Duckling

Our domestic ducklings are produced primarily on Long Island but are available throughout the country. This is a particularly appealing holiday or company selection.

1 duckling, 4-to-5 pounds, cut into quarters
Salt, pepper to taste
1 tablespoon vegetable oil
½ pound fresh mushrooms, cleaned and sliced
1 tablespoon fresh lemon juice

3 tablespoons flour
1½ cups orange juice
1½ cups plain yogurt
1 tablespoon minced orange peel
Salt, pepper to taste
Orange sections
Watercress

Thaw the duckling, if frozen. Wash and pat dry. Sprinkle with salt and pepper. Brown the pieces on all sides in the oil in a skillet. Cook over medium heat, covered, for 30 minutes. Remove the duckling pieces and pour off all except 1 tablespoon of the fat. Sauté the mushrooms in the fat and lemon juice for 3 minutes. Stir in the flour and then add the orange juice and bring to a boil. Lower the heat and slowly add the yogurt. Stir in the orange peel and season with salt and pepper. Cook slowly, covered, about 1¼ hours, or until the duckling is tender. Serve garnished with orange sections and watercress. Serves 4.

Slovenian Chicken Vegetable Paprika

One of Yugoslavia's loveliest republics is northwestern Slovenia, famed as a winter and summer sports area. The Slovene cooking has been influenced by Austria of which it once was a province.

4 slices bacon, chopped
1 large onion, peeled and
    chopped
1 roasting chicken, about 4
    pounds, cleaned,
    washed and wiped dry
Salt, pepper to taste
1 tablespoon paprika
¾ cup scraped and diced
    carrots

1 cup chopped sweet red
    peppers
1 teaspoon hot chili pep-
    pers
1 cup plain yogurt
1 tablespoon wine vinegar
¼ cup chopped fresh pars-
    ley

Cook the bacon in a heavy casserole or kettle. Add the onion and sauté until tender. Rub the chicken with salt and pepper and brown well on all sides. Sprinkle with the paprika. Add 1 cup of water, the carrots and peppers. Cook slowly, covered, about 1 hour, or until the chicken is tender. Remove the chicken to a warm platter and cut into serving pieces. Stir the yogurt, vinegar and parsley into the vegetable mixture and mix well. Heat through and pour over the chicken. Serves 6.

Turkish Pilaf Stuffed Turkey with Yogurt

This well flavored rice or pilaf stuffed turkey is a good buffet specialty.

1 turkey, 8 to 10 pounds
Salt, pepper to taste
8 tablespoons (about) but-
    ter or margarine

1 large onion, peeled and
    minced
2½ cups uncooked long-
    grain rice

4½ cups chicken broth
¼ cup pine nuts
¼ cup currants
1 cinnamon stick

3 tablespoons chopped
fresh parsley
1 cup plain yogurt

Wash the turkey and wipe dry. Sprinkle inside and out with salt and pepper. Melt ⅓ cup of butter in a large skillet. Add the onion and sauté until tender. Add the rice and sauté a few minutes, until the grains become translucent. Pour in the chicken broth and bring to a boil. Lower the heat and add the pine nuts, currants, cinnamon stick, salt and pepper. Cook slowly, covered, about 15 minutes, or until the liquid has been absorbed and the grains are tender. Add the parsley and 2 tablespoons of butter. When slightly cooled, spoon into the turkey cavity. (Set aside any left-over rice to serve later with the turkey.) Sew or close the cavity and truss the turkey. Arrange in a roasting pan. Brush the top with butter and spoon the yogurt over it. Cook in a preheated slow oven (325°F.) about 2½ hours, or until tender. Baste with the juices while cooking. Serves 8 to 10.

Note: The heart, gizzard and liver may be added to the stuffing, if desired. Chop and sauté in butter before adding.

Polynesian Rice Cornish Hens

An interesting and inviting entrée to serve for a special company or holiday dinner.

3 frozen Rock Cornish
hens, about 1½
pounds each
2 tablespoons fresh lemon
juice
2 teaspoons crumbled
dried rosemary
Salt, pepper to taste

1 package (6 ounces)
mixed long-grain and
wild rice
3 green onions, with tops,
minced
1 large green pepper,
cleaned and cubed
2 tablespoons peanut oil

3 water chestnuts, sliced
1-2 tablespoons soy sauce
1 cup drained pineapple
    chunks

2 teaspoons flour
1½ cups plain yogurt at
    room temperature

Thaw hens, split each into 2 halves. Cut off and discard the extra skin around the necks. Sprinkle the skins with the lemon juice, rosemary, salt and pepper. Put, breast sides up, in a buttered shallow baking dish. Roast in a preheated hot oven (450°F.) for 15 minutes. While the hens are roasting partially cook the rice for 15 minutes according to package directions. Reduce the oven to 350°F. and turn the hens over. Spoon the rice into the cavities. Continue cooking for about 35 minutes longer, or until the hens are tender. Remove to a warm platter and keep warm. Have ready a sauce made by sautéeing the onions and peppers in the oil for 3 minutes. Add the water chestnuts, soy sauce and pineapple chunks. Season with salt and pepper. Combine the flour and yogurt and stir into the mixture. Leave on the stove until heated. Serve the sauce with the hens and rice. Serves 6.

Herbed Roast Chicken with Yogurt Sauce

A different way of serving the American favorite, roast chicken.

1 roasting chicken, about 4
    pounds
½ fresh lemon
Salt, pepper to taste
2 tablespoons chopped
    fresh herbs (tarragon,
    parsley, chives, dill,
    basil)

2 tablespoons butter or
    margarine
2 tablespoons flour
1 tablespoon curry powder
Dash paprika
¾ to 1 cup plain yogurt at
    room temperature

Defrost the chicken if frozen. Wash and wipe dry. Rub the skin with the cut lemon and sprinkle with salt and pepper. Put the herbs and butter in the cavity. Truss the chicken and place in a roasting pan. Cover with a sheet of foil and roast in a preheated slow oven (325°F.) for 2½ to 3 hours, until the chicken is cooked. Remove the foil during the last hour of cooking. Remove the chicken to a warm platter and keep warm. Scrape the drippings and add ½ cup of water. Bring to a boil and stir in the flour. Lower the heat and cook slowly, stirring, until thickened. Mix in the curry powder and paprika. Season with salt and pepper. Add more water, if needed, and stir in the yogurt. Leave on the stove long enough to heat through. Serve the sauce with the chicken. Serves 6.

Meats

Americans are hearty meat eaters who relish a wide variety of dishes made with beef, pork, lamb and veal. Cooks around the world have devised so many ingenious ways of preparing these important foods that the repertoire is seemingly endless. Among the most ancient creations were those including yogurt, which was a significant preservative, tenderizer and provider of flavor. We can still enjoy some of these very old culinary contributions as well as many newer ones.

Meat ranks high in our diet and is one of the four food groups necessary for well-balanced meals. It supplies large amounts of protein and is rich in iron and essential B vitamins as well as others. Thus the selection of the various kinds and cuts is important. But fortunately the buyer can rely on the federal stamp and the packer or brand guarantee for assurance of quality products.

Most of our meals are planned around meats and meat products so the knowledge of properly cooking them is all important. A most significant thing to remember is that low heat is the secret to the successful cookery of meat. High temperatures destroy the protein and nutrients, cause toughness and shrinkage and loss of juices. Whether braising, baking, stewing or roasting long slow cooking is recommended. Even in broiling and barbecuing meat which requires higher temperature, the result will be better if the food is placed as far away as possible from the heat and carefully timed so it will not be overcooked.

In ancient times it was necessary to preserve and tenderize meats by various practical methods which early civilizations devised. Middle Easterners discovered that yogurt was an excellent marinade for these purposes and a wide number of interesting dishes were created for beef and lamb specialties. The cooks of Southeast Asian countries also adopted and devised many national favorites which are still staple fare.

The great meat specialties of Eastern Europe such as goulashes, stews and beef stroganoff, prepared traditionally with sour cream, are equally delicious using yogurt. In our country such everyday choices as hamburgers, meat loaves, casseroles and creamed dishes are enhanced by the addition of yogurt, which imparts goodness and flavor to the other ingredients.

Our supermarkets have such a selection of various kinds and cuts of meats and meat products that the buyer could prepare a different creation with them each day of the year. Yet beef is by far the most popular of our meats and the superb roasts, steaks and ground beef are year-round favorites. Pork ranks next in preference and is widely eaten either fresh or cured, as roasts, chops or tenderloins, among others. Not to be forgotten are frankfurters, hams, sausages and spareribs.

Many cooks are experimenting with the preparations of more lamb and veal dishes and the lesser known cuts of beef and veal. Yogurt combines with them all to make an interesting meat repertoire appealing to all tastes for every occasion.

Turkish Shish Kebab with Yogurt Sauce

The famous skewered meat or *shish kebab* has several inviting variations in the Turkish cuisine and this is one of the best.

⅓ cup olive or vegetable oil

3 tablespoons freshly made onion juice

1½ teaspoons crumbled dried thyme

Freshly ground pepper

3 pounds lean lamb, trimmed of fat and cut into 1½ inch cubes

6 large pieces of Arab bread*

1½ cups plain yogurt at room temperature

3 tablespoons melted butter

1 to 2 teaspoons cayenne pepper or paprika

Salt

* Substitute dark toast for the bread, if desired.

Combine the oil, onion juice, thyme and pepper in a large bowl. Add the lamb cubes and mix well. Leave to marinate 1 to 2 hours. Thread the lamb cubes on small skewers and interlard with vegetables (green pepper and onion), if desired. Broil, turning once or twice, about 10 minutes, depending on the desired degree of doneness. Meanwhile, arrange the Arab bread on six plates. Beat the yogurt well and heat over a low fire until just warm. When cooked, remove the lamb cubes from the skewers with a fork onto the bread. Spoon the yogurt over the meat. Combine the butter and cayenne and sprinkle over the yogurt. Season the lamb with salt at the table. Serves 6.

Company Chili Casserole

An easy-to-prepare dish made with favorite south-of-the-border foods.

1 tablespoon vegetable oil
1½ pounds lean ground beef
1 medium onion, peeled and chopped
1 garlic clove, crushed
1½ cups shredded Jack or Cheddar cheese
1 can (15 ounces) enchilada sauce

1 can (1 pound) kidney beans, drained
¾ teaspoon salt
½ to 1 teaspoon chili powder
1 package (6 ounces) corn chips
1 cup plain yogurt at room temperature

Heat the oil in a large skillet. Add the beef, onion and garlic and cook until the beef has lost all its redness. Separate with a fork. Add the cheese, enchilada sauce, beans, salt and chili powder. Place 2 cups of corn chips in a 2-quart casserole. Spoon the beef mixture over them. Bake in a preheated moderate oven (350°F.) for 20 minutes. Spoon the yogurt over the casserole ingredients and cover with the remaining corn chips. Bake about 5 minutes longer, or until the ingredients are cooked. Serves 6 to 8.

Hungarian Pork Tokany

In the Hungarian cuisine a *tokany* is a meat and vegetable dish flavored with paprika and sour cream. This is a good winter supper specialty.

2 pounds lean boneless pork, cut into ¾ inch pieces
¼ cup shortening or oil
Salt, pepper to taste
1 tablespoon paprika
1 large onion, peeled and chopped
3 medium carrots, scraped and sliced
3 medium tomatoes, peeled and chopped
2 cups sliced fresh mushrooms
2 tablespoons butter or margarine
1 tablespoon fresh lemon juice
1 cup plain yogurt at room temperature
2 tablespoons chopped fresh dill

Brown the pork in the shortening in a large saucepan. Season with salt and pepper. Add the paprika and onion and cook until the onion is tender. Cook slowly, covered, about 30 minutes. Add the carrots and tomatoes and cook another 30 minutes, or until the ingredients are tender. Meanwhile, sauté the mushrooms in the butter with the lemon juice for 4 minutes. When the stew is cooked, add the mushrooms, yogurt and dill and leave on the stove long enough to heat through. Serves 6 to 8.

Lebanese Rice Lamb Stuffed Cabbage Leaves

In the Middle Eastern cuisines there are many variations of stuffed cabbage leaves. Each kind is distinguished by the seasonings for the stuffings and the type of sauce. This favorite of Lebanon and Syria is called *mulfoof*.

1 large or 2 small cabbages	*2 tablespoons tomato paste*
1 pound ground lean lamb	*Salt, pepper to taste*
1 cup uncooked long-grain rice	*1 can (1 pound) tomatoes*
½ teaspoon ground cinnamon	*4 fresh mint leaves*
½ teaspoon ground allspice	*Juice of 1 medium lemon*
	1 cup plain yogurt at room temperature

Cut the center hard core from the cabbage or cabbages. Parboil the cabbage in boiling salted water for about 15 minutes, or long enough to soften the leaves. Remove from the water and drain. When slightly cooled, carefully pull off each leaf and cut off any tough veins. Cut the larger leaves into halves. If the inner leaves are not pliable return to the water and cook a little longer.

Combine the lamb, rice, cinnamon, allspice, tomato paste, salt and pepper and mix well. Place a spoonful on each leaf and roll up. Do not wrap too tightly as there must be room for the rice to expand. Put any left-over leaves in a kettle. Arrange the wrapped leaves in layers over them. Put the tomatoes over them. Add the mint leaves and season with salt and pepper. Add also a little water. Cook slowly, covered, about 40 minutes, or until tender. Check to see if more water is needed while cooking. Add the lemon juice and yogurt and cook another 5 minutes. Serve the stuffed cabbage leaves with the sauce in the kettle. Makes about 40.

Barbecue Beef Kabobs in Yogurt Marinade

Cook and serve these kabobs either outdoors or inside. The marinade imparts an interesting flavor to the beef.

1½ pounds boneless beef sirloin or chuck, cut into 1½ inch cubes
1 cup plain yogurt
2 tablespoons grated onion
1 garlic clove, crushed (optional)
½ teaspoon chili powder
½ teaspoon dried oregano or thyme
4 to 6 drops Tabasco sauce
Salt, pepper to taste
Mushroom caps or small whole mushrooms
Green pepper wedges

Put the beef cubes in a large bowl or shallow dish and cover with the yogurt, onion, garlic, chili, oregano, Tabasco, salt and pepper. Leave to marinate for 3 to 4 hours. Turn the meat about now and then. Thread the beef kabobs on skewers alternately with the mushroom caps and green pepper wedges. Brush with the marinade and broil over medium coals on an outdoor grill, turning two or three times, until the desired degree of doneness, or broil in a stove 3 or 4 inches from the heat for about 10 minutes. Serves 6.

Czech Steaks with Caper Yogurt Sauce

The combination of capers and yogurt gives a most pleasing flavor to round steak.

2 pounds round steak, about 1 inch thick, cut into 4 pieces
Salt, pepper to taste
Flour
4 tablespoons butter or margarine
2 medium onions, peeled and chopped
3 to 4 tablespoons drained capers
3 tablespoons prepared sharp mustard
1 cup plain yogurt at room temperature

Pound the steak with a mallet or the edge of a heavy plate to make as thin as possible. Season with salt and pepper and dredge in flour. Melt 2 tablespoons of butter in a large skillet and add the steak. Fry on both sides until the redness disappears. Remove to a plate. Add the remaining butter to the drippings and fry the onions in it. Add the capers, mustard, 1 cup of water and the steak. Cook very slowly, covered, for about 1¼ hours, or until tender. Add a little more water while cooking, if necessary. Remove the steak to a warm platter and keep warm. Scrape the drippings and add the yogurt, mixed with 2 teaspoons flour, to them. Leave on the stove long enough to heat through and spoon over the steaks. Serves 4.

Anatolian Gardeners' Stew with Yogurt

In the gardens of Turkey's Asiatic peninsula called Anatolia extremely flavorful vegetables are grown, which are used in preparing savory stews such as this one, called *turlu*.

2 *medium onions, peeled and sliced*
¼ *cup butter or margarine*
1 *pound lean lamb, trimmed of fat and cubed*
Salt, pepper to taste
2 *medium zucchini, stemmed and sliced*
2 *medium eggplant, stemmed and cubed*

¼ *pound fresh okra, stemmed and cut up*
2 *large tomatoes, peeled and chopped*
2 *tablespoons chopped fresh dill or parsley*
1 *cup plain yogurt at room temperature*

Sauté the onions in the butter in a large kettle until tender. Add the lamb and brown. Season with salt and pepper. Cover with a little water, about ½ cup, and cook slowly, covered, for 1 hour. Add the prepared vegetables and continue to cook slowly, covered, about 30 minutes longer, or until the ingredients are cooked. Stir in the dill and yogurt. Leave on the stove long enough to heat through. Serves 4 to 6.

Transylvanian Szekely Goulash

This pork and sauerkraut goulash derives from Transylvania, once called "the woody and mountainous country" and where hearty fare is highly esteemed. Now the province is partially in Rumania and Hungary.

2 pounds boneless pork, cut into 1½ inch cubes
3 tablespoons shortening or vegetable oil
2 medium onions, peeled and chopped

1 tablespoon paprika
2 pounds sauerkraut, drained
2 teaspoons flour
1 cup plain yogurt at room temperature

Brown the pork in the shortening. Push aside and add the onions. Sauté until tender. Stir in the paprika and cook 1 minute. Add enough water to cover the ingredients and cook 45 minutes. Add the sauerkraut and continue to cook another 30 minutes, or until the meat is tender. Meanwhile, combine the flour and yogurt and add to the goulash. Leave on the stove long enough to heat through. Serve sprinkled with chopped dill, if desired. Serves 6.

Bulgarian Potato Beef Moussaka with Yogurt

A favorite Balkan and Near Eastern casserole is called *moussaka* and made in interesting variations. This is a robust hearty dish, good for a winter meal.

4 medium potatoes, peeled and sliced
¼ cup shortening or vegetable oil
2 medium onions, peeled and chopped
2 garlic cloves, crushed
1 pound lean ground beef

1 can (8 ounces) tomato sauce
¼ teaspoon crushed dried thyme
Salt, pepper to taste
3 tablespoons chopped fresh parsley
2 eggs, beaten

1 cup plain yogurt at room   ¼ cup grated Kasseri or
  temperature   Parmesan cheese

Fry the potatoes in the shortening until soft and golden. Drain and set aside. Sauté the onions and garlic in the drippings until tender. Add the beef and cook, stirring with a fork, until the redness disappears. Add the tomato sauce, thyme, salt and pepper and cook 1 or 2 minutes, uncovered, to blend the flavors. Stir in the parsley. Arrange half the potato slices in a greased shallow baking dish. Cover with the beef-tomato mixture. Top with the remaining potato slices. Combine the beaten eggs and yogurt and pour over the ingredients. Sprinkle with the cheese. Bake in a preheated moderate oven (350°F.) for about 50 minutes, or until the topping is set. To serve, cut into squares. Serves 4.

Note: This dish may also be made with a medium eggplant, peeled and sliced, substituted for the potatoes. Sprinkle the eggplant slices with flour and fry in hot olive or vegetable oil until golden on both sides. Drain and use in the dish instead of the potatoes.

Hawaiian Ham Medley

A flavorful dish featuring ham, pineapple and yogurt.

¼ cup minced green on-   2 tablespoons light brown
  ions, with tops   sugar
⅓ cup minced green pep-   1½ tablespoons vinegar
  per   1½ tablespoons cornstarch
2 tablespoons peanut or   1 tablespoon soy sauce
  vegetable oil   ¼ teaspoon ground ginger
2 cups diced cooked ham   Pepper to taste
1 can (1 lb, 4 ounces)   1 cup plain yogurt at room
  pineapple chunks   temperature

Sauté the onions and pepper in the oil until tender. Add the ham. Drain the liquid from the pineapple and combine with the sugar, vinegar, cornstarch, soy sauce, ginger and pepper. Stir into the ham mixture and cook slowly, stirring, until thickened. Mix in the yogurt and then the pineapple cubes and continue to cook slowly until the ingredients are heated through. Serves 4.

Central European Baked Meatballs in Yogurt Sauce

A good dish for a buffet meal as it can be prepared beforehand.

Meatballs:

1½ pounds ground beef
½ pound ground pork
½ cup dry bread crumbs
½ cup milk or plain yogurt
2 eggs, beaten
4 green onions, with tops, minced

½ teaspoon dried marjoram
Salt, pepper to taste
Flour
Shortening or vegetable oil for frying

Sauce:

2 tablespoons butter or shortening
2 tablespoons flour
1 cup chicken broth

1½ cups yogurt at room temperature
1 tablespoon paprika

Combine the meatball ingredients, except the flour and shortening, and mix well. Shape into 1½ inch balls. Roll each in flour. Heat a little shortening in a frying pan and brown the meatballs in it on all sides. Remove with a slotted spoon to a casserole. Stir the butter for the sauce into the drippings. Mix in the flour. Add the chicken broth and cook, stirring, until a thick sauce. Add the yogurt and paprika and leave on the stove long enough to heat through. Pour over the meatballs. Sprinkle with chopped parsley or dill, if desired. Bake, uncovered, in a preheated moderate oven (350°F.) about 30 minutes, or until the meatballs are cooked. Serves 6.

Syrian Cracked Wheat Kibbe with Yogurt

The national dish of Syria and Lebanon is a combination of ground lamb, cracked wheat (*bulgur*) and seasonings, which is often served with a yogurt sauce. It is a very healthful and tasty entrée.

1½ *cups cracked wheat* (bulgur)	3 *tablespoons chopped pine nuts*
1½ *pounds ground lean lamb*	6 *tablespoons butter or margarine*
¼ *teaspoon ground allspice*	1 *large onion, peeled and chopped*
¼ *teaspoon ground nutmeg*	1½ *cups plain yogurt*
Salt, pepper to taste	1 *tablespoon chopped fresh or 1 teaspoon dried mint*

Soak the cracked wheat in water to cover for 30 minutes. Squeeze dry and combine with the lamb, allspice, nutmeg, salt and pepper. Turn out on a wooden surface and work with the hands to mix the ingredients thoroughly.

Sauté the pine nuts in 3 tablespoons of butter for 1 minute. Remove to a bowl with a slotted spoon. Sauté the onion in the drippings until tender. Shape the cracked wheat-lamb mixture into a loaf and cut in half. Spread evenly one half of the mixture into a shallow round baking dish or pie plate. Top with sautéed pine nuts, onions and butter drippings. Spread the remaining half of the wheat-lamb mixture over them. Dip a knife into cold water and cut lines diagonally across the top to make diamond shapes. Bake in a preheated moderate oven (350°F.) about 30 minutes. Remove from the oven and pour off any fat that might have accumulated. Spread the top with the remaining 3 tablespoons of butter and put in a hot oven (450°F.) for about 10 minutes, until tender and golden on top. Serve with the yogurt and garnished with the parsley. Serve hot or cold. Serves 6.

Nourishing Family Meat Loaf

An innovative recipe for the great family favorite—meat loaf.

2 pounds lean ground beef (or mixture of beef, pork and veal)	½ cup seedless raisins, previously soaked in hot water
2 eggs, slightly beaten	¼ cup minced onion
⅔ cup wheat germ	2 tablespoons chopped parsley
1½ cups whole-wheat bread crumbs	¼ teaspoon dried sage (optional)
⅓ cup chopped nuts (walnuts, almonds or peanuts)	Salt, pepper to taste
	1 cup plain yogurt

Combine all the ingredients in a large bowl and mix well. Shape into a loaf in a loaf pan. Bake in a preheated moderate oven (350°F.) for about 1 hour, or until the ingredients are cooked. Serves 8.

Azerbaidzhani Spinach Veal Stew

The cuisine of Russia's southern province of Azerbaidzhan includes a number of flavorful stews which are well seasoned with herbs. This one includes a very popular trio of favorite ingredients: spinach, yogurt and dill.

2 *pounds veal or lamb shoulder, cut up into 1½ inch cubes*	⅓ *cup tomato paste*
2 *tablespoons vegetable oil*	2 *pounds fresh spinach, cleaned and cut up*
1 *large onion, sliced*	*Water*
½ *cup minced green onions, with tops*	*Salt, pepper to taste*
1 *garlic clove, crushed*	1 *cup plain yogurt*
	1 *to 2 tablespoons chopped fresh dill*

Trim any excess fat from the meat and wipe dry. Brown on all sides in the oil in a kettle. Push aside and add the onions and garlic and sauté until tender. Stir in the tomato paste and spinach and mix well. Add water to cover and season with salt and pepper. Bring to a boil and then lower the heat and cook slowly, covered, for about 1¼ hours or longer, until the meat is cooked. Add a little more water, if needed, during the cooking. When done stir in the yogurt and dill and leave on the stove long enough to heat through. Serves 4.

Beef Stroganoff

This flavorful dish named for a noted Russian gourmet and bon vivant of the Tsarist court, Count Paul Stroganoff, is made traditionally with sour cream and has become an international favorite.

2 *pounds top sirloin of beef*	1 *large onion, peeled and minced*
3 *tablespoons butter or margarine*	3 *tablespoons tomato paste*
	1 *tablespoon prepared mustard*

1 cup beef consommé
Pinch sugar
Salt, pepper to taste

2 teaspoons flour
1 cup plain yogurt at room
temperature

With a sharp knife cut the beef into strips about 3 inches long and ½ inch thick. Brown in the butter in a skillet until the redness disappears. Remove to a plate. Sauté the onion in the drippings and add the tomato paste, mustard, consommé, sugar, salt and pepper. Mix well. Bring to a boil. Lower the heat and cook slowly, covered, for 10 minutes. Add the beef and continue to cook about 10 minutes longer, or until the meat is the desired degree of doneness. Combine the flour and yogurt and stir into the gravy. Leave on the stove long enough to heat through. Serves 6.

Iraqi Lamb Meatballs with Yogurt

Typical dishes of Iraq are well flavored with spices and herbs which are sold widely in aromatic shops and bazaars.

2 pounds ground lamb
2 garlic cloves, crushed
2 eggs
¼ cup tomato paste
¾ cup chopped fresh parsley
½ teaspoon ground cinnamon
½ teaspoon allspice

Salt, pepper to taste
4 slices stale whole wheat bread
Flour
Oil for frying
2 cups plain yogurt at room temperature
2 teaspoons chopped fresh mint or parsley

Combine the lamb, garlic, eggs, tomato paste, parsley, cinnamon, allspice, salt and pepper and mix well. Soak the bread slices in water to cover until soft. Squeeze dry and break into tiny pieces. Add to the lamb mixture. Mix until thoroughly combined. Shape into 2-inch balls and dust with flour. Brown in hot oil in a skillet. Cook slowly, covered, about 30 minutes, or until done. Check now and then and add a little water, while cooking, if necessary. Stir in the yogurt and mint just before serving. Serves 8 to 10.

Swiss Emince de Veau avec Yaourt

This classic Swiss creation, made with strips of tender veal in a flavorful cream sauce, is a favorite restaurant dish, served generally with a type of potato pancake called *rösti*.

2 pounds veal scallops or cutlets
6 tablespoons (about) butter
2 tablespoons minced shallots or green onions

1 cup dry white wine
1½ cups plain yogurt at room temperature
Salt, pepper to taste

Trim any fat from the veal and discard it. Cut the veal into slivers about ¼ inch wide and 2½ inches long. Heat 3 tablespoons of the butter in a skillet and, when foaming, add half the veal slivers. Sauté, mixing about with a fork, about 2 minutes, or until tender. Remove to a plate and keep warm. Add 3 more tablespoons of butter to the skillet and heat. Add the remaining veal and cook in the same way. Remove to a platter. Add the shallots to the drippings and include more butter, if necessary. Sauté for 1 minute, or until tender. Pour in the wine and bring to a boil. Cook over high heat to reduce almost to half. Add the yogurt and turn down the heat. Cook slowly for 1 minute. Add the veal and any juices and leave on the stove long enough to heat through. Season with salt and pepper. Serves 4 to 6.

Russian Meat Cutlets with Yogurt Sauce

A type of hamburger called *kotlety* is a great Russian favorite for everyday meals.

3 slices stale crusty white
    bread
Water or milk
1 pound lean ground beef,
    veal or pork
1 small onion, minced

1 egg, slightly beaten
Salt, pepper to taste
Fine dry bread crumbs
Oil or butter for frying
¼ cup plain yogurt at
    room temperature

Soak the bread in water or milk to cover. Squeeze dry and break into tiny pieces. Put in a bowl and add the meat, onion, egg, salt and pepper. Mix well to combine the ingredients thoroughly. Shape into thin patties and put in fine dry bread crumbs to cover on all sides. Fry in oil or butter until the ingredients are cooked and the outside is golden and crisp. Remove to a warm plate and keep warm. Stir the yogurt into the drippings until heated. Spoon over the cutlets. Serves 4.

Iranian Yogurt Khoreshe

In Iran a *khoreshe* is a stew-like sauce, made with meat or poultry and fruit or vegetables with seasonings, which is served with rice. It is traditional and everyday fare made in great variation. This good one features yogurt or *mast*.

1 pound boneless shoulder
    of lamb or veal, cut
    into 1-inch cubes and
    trimmed of excess fat
2 tablespoons vegetable oil
1 medium onion, peeled
    and chopped
½ teaspoon turmeric pow-
    der

½ teaspoon ground cori-
    ander
2 cardamom seeds, pods re-
    moved and crushed
Salt, pepper to taste
1 cup plain yogurt at room
    temperature
1 teaspoon dried or 1 table-
    spoon chopped fresh
    mint

Brown the lamb or veal in the oil in a large saucepan. Push aside and add the onion. Sauté until tender. Mix in the turmeric, coriander, cardamom, salt and pepper and cook about 1 minute. Add water to cover and cook slowly, covered, for 50 to 60 minutes, until the meat is tender. Check during the cooking to see if additional water is needed. Stir in the yogurt and mint and leave on the stove long enough to heat through. Serves 4.

Southern Sausage Supper

Serve this tomato-sausage dish with hot hominy grits or rice.

2 pounds pork sausage meat	½ teaspoon crumbled dried oregano or thyme
1 cup diced green pepper	
1 cup diced celery	Salt, pepper to taste
1 cup diced onion	2 tablespoons flour
2 cans (1 pound each) to- matoes, undrained	1½ cups plain yogurt
	2 tablespoons chopped fresh parsley
½ teaspoon dried basil	

Cook the sausage meat, separating with a fork, until the redness disappears. Drain off all except 2 tablespoons of the fat. Push aside the meat and add the green pepper, celery and onion and sauté in the fat for 3 or 4 minutes. Add the tomatoes and break them up into fine pieces. Stir in the basil, oregano, salt and pepper. Cook slowly, covered, for about 25 minutes, or until the ingredients are tender. Combine the flour, yogurt and parsley and mix into the sausage mixture. Continue to cook slowly about 5 minutes longer. Serves 8.

Lamb Korma from Kashmir

This is an adaptation of a traditional lamb-yogurt dish popular in northern India.

1½ pounds lean boneless leg or shoulder of lamb or sirloin or chuck beef, cut into 1½ inch cubes
1 cup plain yogurt
½ teaspoon ground cinnamon
½ teaspoon ground coriander
½ teaspoon ground caraway
2 cardamom seeds, pods removed and crushed
Salt, pepper to taste
1 large onion, peeled and chopped
1 garlic clove, crushed
2 tablespoons butter or vegetable oil
2 teaspoons turmeric powder
1 teaspoon minced fresh ginger (optional)
2 large tomatoes, peeled and chopped

Marinate the lamb or beef in the yogurt, cinnamon, coriander, caraway, cardamom, salt and pepper for 6 hours or overnight. Sauté the onion and garlic in the butter until tender. Mix in the turmeric powder, ginger and tomatoes and cook, stirring, for 1 or 2 minutes. Break up the tomatoes with a spoon. Add the meat and yogurt marinade and cook slowly, covered, for about 1½ hours, or until the meat is tender. Serves 6.

Herbed Wheat Germ Hamburgers in Yogurt Sauce

These nourishing hamburgers are one more innovative way of serving these all-American favorites.

2 pounds ground lean beef
¼ cup minced green onions, with tops
¾ teaspoon each of crumbled dried savory and thyme
⅓ cup chopped fresh parsley
3 tablespoons wheat germ
1 egg, slightly beaten
Salt, pepper to taste
2 to 3 tablespoons vegetable oil
1½ cups plain yogurt at room temperature
½ cup ketchup

Combine the first six ingredients in a bowl. Season with salt and pepper. Shape into 8 hamburger patties and fry in the oil in a large skillet. Cook, turning occasionally, until just done. Add the yogurt and ketchup and cook slowly, covered, 5 minutes to blend the flavors. Serves 8.

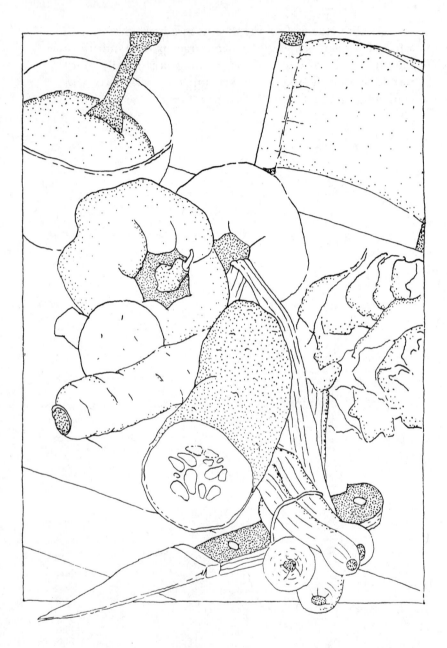

Salads and Vegetables

Among the many gastronomic treats which feature yogurt, salads and vegetables are of utmost significance and appeal. The possibilities are so fascinating to explore, and pleasurable to enjoy, that it is very difficult to choose a representative selection of the many inviting creations which can be prepared and served in various roles with our meals or as snacks in between them.

Our salads, of course, may be made with one or more greens, vegetables, fruits and/or other foods in various forms. Most of them are enhanced with the addition of dressings and sauces. Although they are generally served as an accompaniment to main courses, they may be also offered as appetizers, separate courses, or, on some occasions, as desserts.

The preparation of either raw or cooked ingredients should be done with care and devotion or the result can be very distasteful. Salad greens should be as fresh as possible, washed thoroughly, and completely dried so the flavor and nutrients are not lost or diminished. The tossing of a salad made with greens and other vegetables or foods is not to be taken lightly and should be done just before serving. Some other kinds of salads can be prepared beforehand and refrigerated.

We are indeed fortunate in the bountiful supply of vegetables, either fresh, canned, frozen or dried, which our stores and markets display, but too often our selection is limited to only a few familiar kinds. Cooks could vary their menus considerably by taking the time and effort to investigate the pleasure of cooking and eating such good but lesser known vegetables as artichokes, red cabbages, celery roots, rutabagas, parsnips and zucchini.

All vegetables, however, should be prepared and cooked properly or they lose their flavor, color and nutrient values. A primary rule to

remember is that they should never be soaked in water as their goodness passes into the liquid. Likewise vegetables should not be boiled in
water which is then discarded, but should be steamed in a small
amount of liquid which is then served with them. Unless the skins are
hard or inedible many of these foods do not have to be peeled before
cooking for a great deal of the desirable goodness is in the skins.

Because vegetables provide us with desirable vitamins A and C
as well as other vitamins and minerals, they should be treated so as
to preserve their maximum value. It is intriguing to discover how
pleasant and attractive an old favorite, such as an onion or potato,
can be when cooked in a new fashion. Yogurt provides flair and flavor
not only to many familiar dishes but to others from the cuisines of
faraway countries. Whenever and however served each will be a rewarding dish.

California Avocado Yogurt Mold

A good salad for a summer ladies' luncheon.

1 package (3 ounces) lime
   flavor gelatin
1 medium ripe avocado,
   halved and peeled
1 tablespoon fresh lemon
   juice
½ teaspoon salt
1 cup plain yogurt
¾ cup cottage cheese
1 large orange, peeled, sec-
   tioned and diced
⅓ cup chopped pecans

Put the gelatin into a large bowl and pour 1 cup boiling
water over it. Stir until dissolved. Chill until partially set.
Mash the avocado and add the lemon juice and salt. Fold
the avocado mixture, yogurt, cottage cheese, diced oranges
and pecans into the gelatin and turn into a 4 cup salad mold.
Chill until firm. Serves 6.

Yogurt Honey Waldorf Salad

An interesting version of a long time American favorite.

3 cups diced unpeeled red
    apples
1 tablespoon fresh lemon
    juice
1 cup diced celery

½ cup chopped raisins
½ cup chopped walnuts
2 tablespoons honey
1 cup plain yogurt
Salt, pepper to taste

Combine the apples, lemon juice, celery, raisins, and walnuts in a bowl. Mix together the honey, yogurt, salt and pepper and pour over the apple mixture. Toss to mix. Chill. Serves 6.

Oriental Bean Sprout Vegetable Salad

A nourishing and tasteful salad featuring bean sprouts.

2 cups drained canned
    bean sprouts
¼ cup thinly sliced white
    or red radishes
1 medium cucumber,
    peeled and sliced
    thinly
6 green onions, with tops,
    sliced

2 medium carrots, scraped
    and sliced thinly
1 medium green pepper,
    cleaned and cut into
    slivers
1 tablespoon soy sauce
1 cup plain yogurt
Salt, pepper to taste

Combine the first six ingredients in a bowl. Mix together the soy sauce, yogurt, salt and pepper and add to the vegetables. Toss lightly. Serves 4 to 6.

Near Eastern Beet Yogurt Salad

A colorful and flavorful easy way to prepare salad.

2 cups sliced cooked or
    canned beets, drained
2 tablespoons wine vinegar
2 teaspoons prepared
    horseradish

1 teaspoon sugar
⅓ to ½ cup plain yogurt
Salt, pepper to taste

Combine the ingredients and chill. Serves 4.

Summer Potato Salad

A good salad for either an indoor or outdoor meal.

4 cups diced cooked po-
tatoes
½ cup chopped celery
¼ cup chopped green pep-
per
¼ cup chopped onion
2 teaspoons prepared
horseradish

2 teaspoons prepared sharp
mustard
1 cup plain yogurt
2 tablespoons chopped
fresh parsley
Salt, pepper to taste
Paprika

Combine the first four ingredients in a large bowl. Mix together the horseradish, mustard, yogurt, parsley, salt and pepper and pour over the vegetables. Toss to blend the ingredients. Cover and chill. Garnish with paprika. Serves 4 to 6.

Caucasian Radish Cucumber Salad

A favorite summer salad from the Caucasus.

2 medium cucumbers,
peeled and sliced
thinly
12 red radishes, washed
and sliced
1 cup sliced green onions

Pinch sugar
Salt, pepper to taste
½ to ¾ cup plain yogurt
Chopped fresh mint or
parsley

Combine the first 3 ingredients in a bowl. Mix together the sugar, salt, pepper and yogurt and spoon over the vegetables. Chill. Serve garnished with the mint or parsley. Serves 4.

Yogurt Spinach Salad

A nourishing and attractive salad.

1 pound fresh spinach,
    washed dried and
    chopped
2 hard-cooked eggs, shelled
    and sliced
4 tablespoons wheat germ
    (optional)

6 slices bacon, cooked and
    crumbled
1 garlic clove, crushed
    (optional)
Salt, pepper to taste
1 cup plain yogurt

Combine all the ingredients and toss lightly. Chill. Serves 6.

Swedish Potato Salad

Another good potato salad recipe which includes beets and capers.

6 medium (about 2
    pounds) potatoes,
    washed
1 medium onion, peeled
    and chopped
1 cup chopped cooked
    beets

2 tablespoons drained ca-
    pers
½ cup mayonnaise
½ cup plain yogurt
Salt, pepper to taste
3 tablespoons chopped
    fresh dill or parsley
Lettuce leaves (optional)

Cook the potatoes in boiling salted water until just tender. Cool, peel and slice. Mix with the remaining ingredients, except the parsley and lettuce. Chill and serve cold on the lettuce leaves, if desired, and garnished with the parsley. Serves 4 to 6.

Lettuce Yogurt Salad From Norway

This salad is made traditionally with sour cream but yogurt is an appealing substitute.

1 small head lettuce
1/4 cup (about) plain yo-
    gurt
1 teaspoon sugar
2 teaspoons cider or wine
    vinegar

1/4 teaspoon prepared mus-
    tard
Salt, pepper to taste
1 hard-cooked egg, shelled
    and cut into wedges

Wash the lettuce. Drain and dry well. Tear into bite-size pieces and put in a large salad bowl. Combine the yogurt, sugar, vinegar, mustard, salt and pepper and mix with the lettuce, tossing lightly. Add more yogurt, if desired. Serve garnished with the eggs. Serves 4.

Swiss Cheese Salad

An innovative salad to serve for a luncheon with cold cuts.

3/4 pound Swiss or Emmen-
    taler cheese, cut into
    1/2 inch cubes
1 medium onion, peeled
    and chopped
1 tablespoon grated horse-
    radish

1/2 cup plain yogurt
2 teaspoons prepared sharp
    mustard
Salt, pepper to taste
Lettuce leaves
Garnishes: tomato slices,
    gherkin slices

Combine the cheese and onion in a bowl. Mix together the horseradish, yogurt and mustard. Season with salt and pepper. Stir into the cheese mixture. Serve spooned onto lettuce leaves and garnished with the tomato and gherkin slices. Serves 4.

Apple Celery Coleslaw

This is an interesting variation of the traditional cabbage salad which is rich in minerals and vitamins.

1 cup plain yogurt
1 tablespoon fresh lemon
    juice
2 teaspoons celery seed
2 tablespoons chopped
    chives

Salt, pepper to taste
1 large apple, unpeeled
    and chopped
4 cups shredded green cab-
    bage
½ cup chopped celery.

Combine the first four ingredients. Season with salt and pepper. When ready to serve, combine the apple, cabbage and celery and pour the sauce over them. Serves 6 to 8.

Viennese Creamed Spinach

Serve with pork or poultry.

2 packages (10 ounces
    each) fresh spinach,
    washed and trimmed
2 tablespoons butter or
    margarine
1 small onion, peeled and
    minced
2 tablespoons flour

½ cup beef bouillon
1 tablespoon fresh lemon
    juice
2 teaspoons chopped fresh
    dill
Salt, pepper to taste
½ cup plain yogurt at
    room temperature

Cook the spinach in a very small amount of salted water until tender. Drain and chop. Melt the butter in a large sauce-pan. Add the onion and sauté until tender. Stir in the flour and cook 1 minute. Gradually add the bouillon and cook, stirring, until thickened. Mix in the chopped cooked spin-ach, lemon juice, dill, salt and pepper, and stir together. Add the yogurt and leave on the stove long enough to heat through. Serves 4.

Indian Spicy Vegetables with Yogurt

Serve with roast lamb or shish kebab.

4 *medium potatoes*
2 *tablespoons vegetable oil*
1 *small onion, peeled and chopped*
1 *garlic clove, crushed*
2 *teaspoons turmeric powder*
1 *teaspoon chili powder*
½ *teaspoon ground coriander*
½ *teaspoon ground cumin*
Salt, pepper to taste
3 *medium tomatoes, peeled and chopped*
1½ *cups cooked green peas*
1 *cup plain yogurt*
2 *tablespoons chopped fresh coriander or parsley*

Wash the potatoes and cook in boiling salted water to cover until tender. Drain, peel and cut into small cubes. Heat the oil in a skillet or saucepan and add the onion and garlic. Sauté until tender. Stir in the turmeric, chili, coriander and cumin. Season with salt and pepper. Cook 1 minute. Add the potatoes and cook until well coated with the spices. Mix in the tomatoes and sauté about 1 minute. Stir in the peas, yogurt and coriander and leave on the stove long enough to heat through. Serves 4.

Balkan Sautéed Carrots

Serve with pork, poultry or lamb.

1 *pound carrots, about 9 medium, washed and scraped*
Flour
Salt, pepper to taste.
¼ *cup butter or margarine*
½ *cup plain yogurt*
2 *tablespoons chopped fresh dill or chives*

Wipe dry the carrots and cut into julienne strips. Dredge in flour seasoned with salt and pepper. Sauté in butter or margarine until tender and golden on the outside, turning now and then. Serve covered with the yogurt and garnished with the dill. Serves 4.

Pakistani Eggplant with Yogurt

Serve with lamb or beef patties or meat loaf.

1 medium eggplant,
    washed and unpeeled
Salt
½ cup (about) olive or
    vegetable oil

1 teaspoon chili powder
1 garlic clove, crushed
Salt, pepper to taste
1 cup plain yogurt

Cut the eggplant into small cubes and put in a colander. Sprinkle with salt and leave over a saucepan or in the sink to drain for 30 minutes. Wipe dry and sauté in the oil until tender and golden. Remove from the heat and mix with the remaining ingredients. Chill. Serves 6.

Rumanian Creamed Mushrooms

Serve with roast beef or steak.

1 pound fresh mushrooms
¼ cup butter or margarine
½ cup minced green on-
    ions, with tops
1 tablespoon fresh lemon
    juice

Dash nutmeg
Salt, pepper to taste
¼ cup flour
½ cup milk
1 cup plain yogurt at room
    temperature

Wash the mushrooms quickly or wipe any dirt from them with wet paper toweling. Cut lengthwise into slices. Heat the butter in a large skillet and sauté the onions in it until tender. Add the mushroom slices and lemon juice and sauté for 4 minutes. Season with nutmeg, salt and pepper. Stir in the flour and then gradually add the milk. Mix well and cook 1 minute. Gradually add the yogurt and leave on the stove just long enough to heat through. Serves 4.

Southern Honey Yogurt Sweet Potatoes

Serve with baked ham or pork chops.

4 medium sweet potatoes,
   peeled, cooked and
   mashed
2 tablespoons butter or
   margarine
¼ cup honey

½ teaspoon nutmeg or
   cinnamon
⅓ to ½ cup plain yogurt
   at room temperature
Salt, pepper to taste

Combine the mashed potatoes while still warm with the remaining ingredients and spoon into a shallow baking dish. Put under the broiler for a few minutes, long enough to heat the ingredients. Serves 4.

Zucchini with Yogurt Italiano

Serve with roast veal, veal cutlets or seafood.

1 large onion, peeled and
   sliced
1 garlic clove, crushed
3 tablespoons olive or vegetable oil
1 can (6 ounces) tomato
   paste

3 medium zucchini,
   washed and diced
½ teaspoon dried basil
½ teaspoon dried oregano
Salt, pepper to taste
½ cup plain yogurt at
   room temperature

Sauté the onion and garlic in the oil until tender. Add the tomato paste, zucchini, basil, oregano, salt and pepper and thin with water to the desired consistency. Cook slowly, covered, for about 10 minutes, or until the zucchini is tender. Stir in the yogurt and leave on the stove another 5 minutes. Serves 4.

Barbecue Yogurt Kidney Beans

Serve with grilled hamburgers, steaks or chicken halves.

2 medium onions, peeled
   and chopped

1 garlic clove, crushed
2 tablespoons olive or vegetable oil

2 large tomatoes, peeled and chopped
1 medium green pepper, cleaned and chopped
1 to 2 teaspoons chili powder
½ teaspoon dried oregano

Salt, pepper to taste
4 cups canned kidney beans, drained
1 cup plain yogurt at room temperature
¼ cup chopped fresh parsley

Sauté the onions and garlic in the oil until tender. Add the tomatoes, green pepper, chili powder, oregano, salt and pepper and cook slowly, uncovered, for 15 minutes. Stir in the kidney beans and cook slowly, covered, for 10 minutes. Add the yogurt and parsley and leave on the stove long enough to heat through. Serves 4.

Bohemian Sweet Sour Red Cabbage

Serve with roast pork, chicken or game.

1 medium head red cabbage
3 tablespoons butter or margarine
1 large tart red apple, peeled and chopped
½ cup cider vinegar

3 tablespoons sugar
¼ teaspoon caraway or dill seed
Salt, pepper to taste
1 tablespoon flour
¾ cup plain yogurt at room temperature

Core and shred the cabbage. Melt the butter in a saucepan and sauté the cabbage in it for 5 minutes. Add the remaining ingredients, except the flour and yogurt, and cook slowly for 30 minutes, or until the cabbage is tender. Combine the flour and yogurt and stir into the cooked cabbage. Leave on the stove long enough to heat through, stirring while heating. Serves 4.

Albanian Fried Squash with Yogurt

Serve with fish, poultry or lamb.

2 pounds yellow summer
    squash
Fine dry bread crumbs
2 eggs, beaten
Olive or vegetable oil for
    frying

1 cup plain yogurt
1 garlic clove, crushed
2 tablespoons chopped
    fresh mint

Wash the squash and remove the stem. Cut, unpeeled, crosswise into slices. Dip in bread crumbs, then in beaten egg, and again in bread crumbs. Heat $1/8$ of a cup of oil in a skillet and fry the squash slices until crisp and golden on both sides. Drain on absorbent paper. Combine the yogurt, garlic and mint and serve with the squash. Serves 4 to 6.

Turkish Rice Filled Tomatoes

Serve these flavorful stuffed tomatoes with roast beef or lamb, or with sliced cold cooked meat or poultry for a buffet.

12 to 14 medium tomatoes
Salt
$1/2$ cup olive or vegetable
    oil
1 cup finely chopped on-
    ions
$1/3$ cup chopped pine nuts
1 cup long grain rice
2 cups chicken bouillon or
    water

$1/3$ cup chopped currants
$1/2$ teaspoon nutmeg
Pepper to taste
$1/3$ cup chopped fresh pars-
    ley
2 cups plain yogurt
2 garlic cloves, crushed
Cayenne pepper

Cut a slice from the stem end of each unpeeled tomato. Set aside the slices. Carefully spoon out all the pulp. Sprinkle the insides with salt, and invert to drain. Heat $1/4$ cup of the oil in a skillet. Add the onions and sauté until tender. Add the pine nuts and rice and sauté until the grains are translucent and well coated with oil. Add the bouillon and bring to a boil. Mix in the currants and nutmeg. Season with salt and pepper. Cook, uncovered, briskly for 10 minutes, until just about all the liquid is absorbed and the grains are tender. Remove from the heat and stir in the parsley. Spoon into the tomato shells, filling loosely. Cover with the stem slices and place in a large kettle. Add 1/4 cup of olive oil and a little water. Cook slowly, covered, about 30 minutes, until tender. Carefully remove with a slotted spoon and serve with the yogurt, garlic and cayenne, seasoned with salt and pepper, in a bowl. Serves 12 to 14.

Yogurt Baked Potatoes

Scrub 1 large potato for each person and rub with butter or margarine. Bake in a preheated hot oven (450°F.) for about 45 minutes, or until done. Cut a cross in the top of each and press at the bottom to push up the cooked potato. Put a small square of butter in the cut section. Season with salt and pepper. Serve a small bowl of plain yogurt and garnishes of red caviar, chopped chives or green onions, crumbled crisp bacon or chopped parsley with the potatoes.

Hungarian Potato Paprikas

Serve with pork, veal or beef.

2 medium onions, peeled
    and chopped
2 garlic cloves, crushed
3 tablespoons bacon drippings or shortening
1 to 2 tablespoons paprika

Salt, pepper to taste
6 medium potatoes, peeled
    and cubed
1 cup plain yogurt at room
    temperature

Sauté the onions and garlic in the hot drippings in a saucepan or skillet. Stir in the paprika, salt and pepper and cook 1 minute. Add the potatoes and enough water to barely cover. Cook slowly, covered, for about 15 minutes, or until the potatoes are just cooked. Stir in the yogurt and leave over low heat long enough to warm through. Serves 4 to 6.

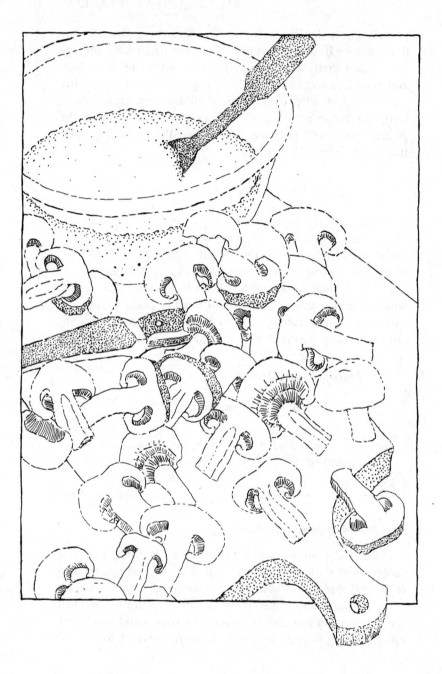

Dressings and Sauces

Simple or complex, thin or thick, cold or hot, sweet or sour, dressings and sauces are very important to our cookery and there is a wide range of them.

The art of making dressings and sauces is very ancient and was born of necessity. For early man devised them not only to augment other foods but to act as preservatives, particularly in hot climates.

Probably the world's first sauces were those created in the Indus Valley of what is now the country of Pakistan. Eventually these spicy mixtures, to which yogurt was added, became known internationally as curries and are still essential to the cuisines of many Asiatic countries.

Near Easterners began making dressings with honey, wine or vinegar, herbs, spices, onions and garlic. Very important to the early mixtures also were olive oil, the oil and seeds of sesame, and yogurt, all of which are still staple fare in these lands.

Over the centuries, as the knowledge of cookery and gastronomy increased, the art of sauce-making developed considerably and the triumph of many a dish was attributed to it. The French cooks in particular created many classic creations which have been adopted and made a part of several Western cuisines.

Today it is almost impossible to serve a meal without such kitchen staples as mayonnaise, French dressing, and white or brown sauce, which can be either purchased or made at home. Variations of these can be made with yogurt into very appealing and different culinary treats.

With yogurt the homemaker can easily devise impromptu dressings and sauces to serve with fruit or vegetable salads, cooked eggs, pasta, poultry, seafood, meats and vegetables. For it is only necessary to add any of a number of flavorings or seasonings to the plain yogurt. Among these could be chopped herbs, onions, capers, vegetables, olives, pickles, nuts, or raisins; sweet relish, honey, shredded coconut; or cut-up or puréed fruit. Yogurt can also be mixed with any of the excellent varied condensed soups to make an inviting sauce. Included below are more specific suggestions primarily designed to enhance the enjoyment of particular categories of dishes but also capable of wider application.

Watercress Yogurt Dressing

A good dressing for a seafood or shrimp cocktail.

½ cup mayonnaise
¼ cup ketchup
2 teaspoons fresh lemon
   juice

2 teaspoons prepared
   horseradish
Salt, pepper to taste
1 cup plain yogurt
1 cup chopped watercress

Combine the ingredients, except the watercress, and chill. Stir in the watercress before serving. Makes about 2¾ cups sauce.

Yogurt Mayonnaise

Serve with salads, cooked fish, meat or vegetables.

1 cup plain yogurt
½ cup mayonnaise

2 teaspoons sugar
Salt, pepper to taste

Combine the ingredients and chill. Makes about 1½ cups.

Note: Vary by adding chopped herbs, ketchup, capers, sliced olives or pickle relish.

Blue Cheese Dressing

Serve with salad greens or cooked vegetables.

1/4 cup crumbled Blue
   cheese
1 teaspoon lemon juice or
   vinegar

1 teaspoon Worcestershire
   sauce (optional)
1/2 teaspoon sugar
Salt, to taste
1 cup plain yogurt

Combine the ingredients and chill. Makes about 1¼ cups.

Yogurt Tartare Sauce

Serve with fish.

1/2 cup mayonnaise
1/2 cup plain yogurt
2 tablespoons minced
   green pepper
2 tablespoons minced
   sweet pickle

1 tablespoon minced onion
1 tablespoon minced fresh
   parsley
1 tablespoon capers
Salt, pepper to taste

Combine the ingredients and mix well. Chill. Makes about 1½ cups.

Vegetable Salad Dressing

Serve with cooked vegetables or salad greens.

1 cup plain yogurt
1 small onion, minced
1/4 cup chopped celery
   leaves

2 teaspoons cider vinegar
Salt, pepper to taste

Combine the ingredients and chill. Makes about 1¼ cups.

Hungarian Salad Dressing

Serve with sliced or chopped cucumbers, tomatoes or lettuce leaves.

1 cup plain yogurt

1 teaspoon sugar

2 tablespoons wine vinegar

Salt, pepper to taste

3 tablespoons chopped dill

Combine the ingredients and chill. Makes about 1¼ cups.

Yogurt Thousand Island Dressing

Serve with salad greens, cooked eggs, fish or vegetables.

½ cup chili sauce

2 teaspoons chopped chives

2 tablespoons sweet pickle relish

1 teaspoon prepared mustard

2 tablespoons minced onion

½ cup mayonnaise

¾ cup plain yogurt

Combine the ingredients and chill. Makes about 2 cups.

Low Calorie Cottage Cheese Yogurt Dressing

Serve with salad greens or fruits.

1 cup cottage cheese

¼ cup chopped fresh herbs (tarragon, basil, dill, parsley, chives, oregano)

1 tablespoon chopped onion

1 tablespoon fresh lemon juice or tarragon vinegar

1 cup plain yogurt

Salt, pepper to taste

Combine the ingredients and chill. Makes about 2¼ cups.

Walnut Raisin Fruit Dressing

Serve with plain fruits or fruit salads.

1 cup plain yogurt
¼ cup chopped walnuts
¼ cup chopped raisins

3 tablespoons honey or
     maple-flavored syrup

Combine the ingredients and chill. Makes about 1½ cups.

Diet French Dressing with Yogurt

½ cup vegetable oil
½ cup plain yogurt
⅓ cup fresh lemon juice or
     cider vinegar

3 tablespoons tomato juice
     (optional)
2 teaspoons minced onion
Paprika, salt, pepper to
     taste

Combine the ingredients and mix well. Makes about 1⅓ cups.

Yogurt Fresh Mint Dressing

Serve with cottage cheese, fruits, or cooked lamb.

½ cup chopped fresh mint
     leaves
2 teaspoons sugar

1 tablespoon fresh lemon
     juice or vinegar
Salt, pepper to taste
1 cup plain yogurt

Crush the mint leaves and mix with the sugar, lemon juice, salt and pepper. Fold in the yogurt. Chill. Makes about 1¼ cups.

Yogurt Honey Fruit Dressing

Serve with fruit salad.

¼ cup honey
½ cup crushed pineapple,
     drained

¼ cup shredded coconut
1 cup plain yogurt

Combine the ingredients and chill. Makes about 2 cups.

Yogurt Dressing Niçoise

Serve with salad greens, cooked eggs or fish.

1 cup plain yogurt
1 small onion, peeled and
   minced
1 garlic clove, crushed
1 large tomato, peeled and
   chopped

¼ cup sliced green, black
   or stuffed olives
½ teaspoon crumbled
   dried oregano or basil
Salt, pepper to taste

Combine the ingredients and chill. Makes about 1¼ cups.

Bulgarian Yogurt Sauce

Serve with cooked vegetables, fish or meat.

2 cups plain yogurt at
   room temperature
¼ cup hot beef bouillon
Salt, pepper to taste
1 or 2 garlic cloves,
   crushed

2 tablespoons butter or
   margarine
1 teaspoon paprika
2 tablespoons chopped
   fresh dill or parsley

Heat the yogurt over a low fire. Add the bouillon, salt, pepper and garlic and heat through. Combine the butter, paprika and dill and stir into the hot yogurt mixture just before serving. Makes about 2¼ cups.

Cucumber Yogurt Sauce à la Russe

Serve with cooked fish or vegetables.

3 tablespoons butter or
   margarine
1 cup diced peeled cucum-
   ber

1 tablespoon flour
½ cup vegetable bouillon
   or ½ vegetable bouil-
   lon cube and ½ cup
   water

½ cup plain yogurt at
  room temperature
1 tablespoon fresh lemon
  juice

2 tablespoons chopped
  fresh dill

Melt the butter in a saucepan. Add the cucumber and sauté until tender. Stir in the flour. Pour in the bouillon and cook, stirring, until thickened. Mix in the yogurt, lemon juice and chopped dill and leave on the stove just long enough to heat through. Makes about 1¼ cups.

Tomato Yogurt Sauce from Italy

Serve with cooked pasta, beef or poultry.

1 large onion, peeled and
  chopped
1 or 2 garlic cloves,
  crushed
2 tablespoons olive or salad
  oil
2 teaspoons crumbled
  dried herbs (basil,
  thyme, marjoram, ore-
  gano)

1 bay leaf
1 can (6 ounces) tomato
  paste
1 can (1 pound) tomatoes
Salt, pepper to taste
2 teaspoons flour
1 cup plain yogurt at room
  temperature
2 tablespoons chopped
  fresh parsley

Sauté the onion and garlic in the oil in a medium saucepan or skillet until tender. Mix in the herbs and bay leaf and sauté 1 minute. Add the tomato paste, 1 can of water and the tomatoes. Mix well and break up the tomatoes into small pieces. Season with salt and pepper and cook slowly uncovered, for 30 minutes. Remove and discard the bay leaf. Mix in the flour, yogurt and parsley and cook over low heat another 1 or 2 minutes, or until warmed through. Makes 4 cups.

Hungarian Dill Yogurt Sauce

Serve with cold cooked meat, poultry or fish.

2 tablespoons butter or
   margarine
1 medium onion, peeled
   and chopped
2 tablespoons flour
Salt, pepper to taste

2 cups hot chicken broth
Juice of ½ lemon
½ cup plain yogurt at
   room temperature
2 tablespoons chopped
   fresh dill

Melt the butter in a saucepan and sauté the onion in it until tender. Mix in flour and cook 1 minute, stirring constantly. Season with salt and pepper. Add the hot broth and cook slowly, stirring constantly, until thickened. Stir in the lemon juice, yogurt and dill and leave on the stove just long enough to heat through. Makes about 2½ cups.

Mushroom Yogurt Sauce

Serve with cooked pasta, meat or poultry.

1 small onion or 3 green
   onions, peeled and
   minced
¼ cup butter or margarine
2 cups sliced fresh mush-
   rooms
1 tablespoon fresh lemon
   juice

Salt, pepper to taste
2 tablespoons flour
1 cup vegetable or beef
   bouillon
½ cup plain yogurt at
   room. temperature.
Dash cayenne or paprika

Sauté the onion in the butter in a saucepan until tender. Add the mushrooms and lemon juice and sauté 4 minutes. Season with salt and pepper. Stir in the flour and mix well. Slowly add the bouillon and cook, stirring often, about 5 minutes, or until thickened. Stir in the yogurt and cayenne and leave on the stove long enough to heat through. Makes about 2 cups.

Easy Yogurt Honey Sauce

Serve with fruit.

Combine ⅔ cup yogurt, ⅓ cup unsweetened pineapple or orange juice and 2 tablespoons honey. Makes about 1 cup.

Cheese Yogurt Sauce from Holland

Serve with cooked eggs, pasta or vegetables.

3 tablespoons butter or
    margarine
3 tablespoons flour
¾ cup hot milk
¾ cup plain yogurt at
    room temperature

1 cup grated Gouda or
    Edam cheese
1 teaspoon prepared sharp
    mustard
¼ teaspoon paprika
Salt, pepper to taste

Melt the butter in a saucepan and stir in the flour. Cook 1 minute. Gradually add the milk and then the yogurt and cook slowly, stirring, until thickened and smooth. Mix in the cheese, mustard, paprika, salt and pepper and cook slowly, stirring, until the cheese melts. Makes about 2 cups.

Viennese Caper Yogurt Sauce

Serve with cooked fish, pork or poultry.

¼ cup butter or margarine
3 tablespoons flour
1½ cups beef bouillon
½ cup plain yogurt at
    room temperature

2 tablespoons drained ca-
    pers
Salt, pepper to taste

Melt the butter in a saucepan and stir in the flour. Gradually add the bouillon and cook, stirring, over low heat until thickened. Add the yogurt, capers, salt and pepper and cook for 1 minute. Makes about 1¾ cups.

Avocado Yogurt Cocktail Sauce

Serve as a sauce for shrimp or seafood cocktails.

1 medium ripe avocado	1 teaspoon Worcestershire
1 tablespoon fresh lemon	sauce
juice	⅓ to ½ cup plain yogurt
¼ cup chili sauce	Salt, pepper to taste

Peel the avocado and cut in half. Remove the seed and mash or purée. Add the lemon juice and mix well. Combine with the remaining ingredients. Makes about 1½ cups.

Scandinavian Egg Yogurt Sauce

Serve with cooked fish, poultry, eggs or vegetables.

2 tablespoons butter or	4 hard-cooked eggs, shelled
margarine	and chopped
2 tablespoons flour	2 teaspoons fresh lemon
1 cup hot milk	juice
1 cup plain yogurt at room	1 tablespoon chopped fresh
temperature	dill
Salt, pepper to taste	

Melt the butter in a saucepan and stir in the flour. Gradually add the hot milk and cook slowly, stirring, until thickened and smooth. Add the yogurt and continue to cook slowly for about 1 more minute. Season with salt and pepper and stir in the eggs, lemon juice and dill. Leave on the stove long enough to heat through. Makes about 2½ cups.

Seafood Yogurt Tomato Sauce

Serve with cooked seafood.

1 cup tomato sauce
1 tablespoon prepared
    horseradish
1 tablespoon fresh lemon
    juice

½ cup plain yogurt
Few drops Tabasco
Salt, pepper to taste

Combine the ingredients and chill. Makes about 1½ cups.

Baked Goods and Desserts

The culinary roster of baked goods and desserts which can be made with yogurt is an extensive one. Yogurt is an interesting innovation in many familiar breads, cakes, cookies, muffins, pancakes, pies, puddings, fruit and ice cream dishes, as well as those which are lesser known.

Baking is an ancient art. For thousands of years man has been cooking in ovens and over the years his repertoire and expertise have expanded considerably. A very early Near Eastern creation was a cake made with yogurt which is still a favorite in Greece, Turkey and some Balkan countries.

The use of yogurt in the preparation of baked goods, however, has not been widely explored. Thus there is considerable pleasure in making and serving such everyday fare as yogurt whole wheat biscuits or such company fare as Russian yogurt *blini*. Generally speaking, the cultured milk can be substituted for fresh milk, sour cream or buttermilk in baked goods but ½ teaspoon of baking soda should be included for each cup of yogurt.

The contemporary cook can also derive considerable satisfaction in serving yogurt desserts, sometimes as a replacement for oversweet ones. Ancient cooks served yogurt as a topping for fresh or cooked fruits and this is still an excellent idea. Either plain or flavored yogurt may be spooned over baked apples, ice cream, puddings, pancakes, gelatin molds or cakes. Delectable desserts can be easily and quickly made by combining or topping plain yogurt with fruit, honey, maple syrup, preserves, raisins, currants, brown sugar, spices, flaked coconut, chopped nuts or dates.

Many of these yogurt creations can be enjoyed also as snacks or with morning coffee or afternoon tea. A particular favorite for the children can be easily made by freezing flavored or plain yogurt and fruit juice in ice cube trays. Stick a small wooden spoon in each compartment and you will have nutritious popsicles. Yogurt, mixed with puréed fruits and frozen, will make delicious lollipops.

A variety of foods is covered in this selection and each will be a pleasure and perhaps a surprise to serve and savor.

Date Yogurt Muffins with Wheat Germ

The heart and most vital part of the wheat kernel called the germ is a valuable natural food as it contains 30 nutrients. It is extra rich in high-quality protein, iron, the B vitamins and vitamin E. It can be eaten by itself but is also a versatile cooking ingredient.

1½ cups unsifted all-purpose flour	⅓ cup sugar
2 teaspoons baking powder	1 cup chopped dates
1 teaspoon baking soda	⅔ cup plain yogurt
½ teaspoon salt	¼ cup melted shortening or margarine
½ cup wheat germ	2 eggs

Sift the flour, baking powder and soda and salt into a large bowl. Add the wheat germ, sugar and dates and stir well. Mix together the yogurt, shortening and eggs and stir into the flour mixture. Spoon into greased muffin tins, filling about ¾ full. Bake in a preheated hot oven (400°F.) for about 20 minutes, or until cooked. Makes about 1 dozen muffins.

Yogurt Chocolate Cake

This delicious cake is made with yogurt and topped with a chocolate-yogurt glaze.

3 squares (1 ounce each) unsweetened chocolate	½ cup butter or margarine
½ cup water	1 cup sugar
1½ cups plain yogurt	½ cup firmly packed light brown sugar

3 eggs
1 teaspoon vanilla
2 cups sifted cake flour
1 teaspoon baking soda

1 teaspoon salt
1 package (6 ounces) semi-
   sweet chocolate pieces

Melt the chocolate in a heavy saucepan or the top of a
double boiler over low heat. Stir in the water. Remove from
the heat and cool. Mix with 1 cup of yogurt and set aside.
Cream the butter in a large bowl and stir in the sugars. Beat
until light and fluffy. Beat in the eggs one at a time. Add the
vanilla. Sift together the flour, soda and salt, and add to the
creamed mixture alternately with the yogurt mixture. Turn
into a greased and floured baking dish, 13 x 9 x 2 inches, and
bake in a preheated moderate oven (350°F.) for about 35
minutes, or until done. While cooking prepare a glaze by
melting the chocolate pieces in a saucepan, stirring constantly. Remove from the heat and stir in the remaining ½
cup of yogurt. Spread on top of the cake and let it run down
the sides. Serves about 12.

Prune Yogurt Bread

A nutritious bread made with dried plums, or prunes,
which are good sources of iron. Prunes have long been staple
fare in northern Europe and America.

2 cups all-purpose flour
1½ teaspoons baking pow-
   der
1 teaspoon baking soda
1½ teaspoons salt
⅓ cup sugar
1 cup whole-wheat flour
2 eggs, slightly beaten

1 cup plain yogurt
2 tablespoons melted shortening
¼ cup prune juice
1 cup chopped cooked
   prunes
½ cup chopped almonds
   (optional)

Sift the all purpose flour. Add the baking powder and
soda, salt and sugar and sift into a large bowl. Add the whole-
wheat flour and mix well. Combine the eggs, yogurt, melted

shortening and prune juice, and stir into the flour mixture. Add the prunes and the almonds, if used. Stir until the ingredients are combined. Turn into a greased loaf pan and bake in a preheated moderate (350°F.) oven for about 1 hour or until cooked. Serves 8 to 10.

Orange Yogurt Cake

½ cup butter or margarine, softened	1 teaspoon baking powder
1 cup firmly packed light brown sugar	1 teaspoon baking soda
	½ teaspoon salt
2 eggs, slightly beaten	1 cup raisins
¾ cup plain yogurt	1 large orange, juiced
1 cup whole-wheat flour	(about ½ cup)
1 cup all-purpose white flour	2 teaspoons grated orange rind

Cream the butter and sugar in a large bowl. Add the eggs and yogurt and mix well. Sift the whole-wheat and white flour, baking powder and soda, and salt into the creamed mixture and mix well. Add the raisins, orange juice and rind and mix again. Pour into a greased 9 inch square pan and bake in a preheated moderate (375°F.) oven for about 45 minutes, or until done. Serves 8 to 10.

Note: This cake may be frosted with an orange icing, if desired.

Peanut Butter Yogurt Bread

Peanut butter is so commonly used as a spread for bread and crackers that its versatility as a cooking ingredient is sometimes forgotten. It can be used in making many fine desserts and baked goods such as this flavorful bread.

½ cup peanut butter	1 tablespoon melted butter or margarine
⅓ cup sugar	
1 egg	1 cup plain yogurt

1 teaspoon grated orange
   rind
2 cups all-purpose flour
1 teaspoon baking soda

1 teaspoon baking powder
½ teaspoon salt
½ cup chopped peanuts

Combine the peanut butter, sugar and egg in a large bowl and mix well. Stir in the butter, yogurt and orange rind and mix again. Sift the flour, baking soda and powder and salt into the peanut butter mixture and stir to combine the ingredients. Turn into a loaf pan, 9 x 5 x 3, and bake in a preheated moderate oven (350°F.) for about 1 hour, or until done. Cool about 5 minutes and turn out onto a rack. Serves 8 to 10.

Spice Raisin Cake with Yogurt

Some of America's earliest cakes were flavored with spices and raisins. Yogurt adds further appeal to this variation.

½ cup butter or marga-
   rine, softened
1 cup firmly packed light
   brown sugar
1 egg
1 teaspoon vanilla
1 cup plain yogurt
2½ cups all-purpose flour

1 teaspoon ground nutmeg
1 teaspoon ground cinna-
   mon
¼ teaspoon ground cloves
1 teaspoon baking soda
½ teaspoon salt
1 cup seedless raisins

Cream the butter in a large bowl and mix in the sugar. Beat until light and fluffy. Add the egg and vanilla and mix well. Stir in the yogurt. Sift together the flour, nutmeg, cinnamon, cloves, soda and salt into the yogurt mixture. Stir in the raisins. Mix to combine the ingredients. Spoon into a greased 9 inch square pan and bake in a preheated moderate (350°F.) oven about 45 minutes, or until done. Cool 5 minutes and turn out onto a rack. Serves 8 to 10.

Yogurt Whole Wheat Biscuits

A good quick bread to serve for a luncheon.

1 cup all-purpose flour	½ teaspoon salt
1 cup whole wheat flour	6 tablespoons shortening
4 teaspoons baking powder	1 cup plain yogurt
½ teaspoon baking soda	

Sift the flours, baking powder and soda and salt into a large bowl. Cut the shortening into the mixture and stir in the yogurt. Blend the ingredients. Turn out on a floured board and knead several times. Roll lightly to a ½ inch thickness. Cut into 2-inch biscuits. Place on a greased cookie sheet and bake in a preheated hot (475°F.) oven about 15 minutes, or until cooked. Makes about 18 biscuits.

Baked Pancakes from Yugoslavia

This is a good dessert for a company meal. Prepare the pancakes beforehand and spread with yogurt and bake shortly before serving.

2 eggs, beaten slightly	Butter or margarine for frying
1½ cups milk	Fruit jam or jelly
¼ teaspoon salt	Slivered almonds
1 tablespoon sugar	1 cup plain yogurt at room temperature
2 teaspoons grated lemon rind	Confectioners' sugar
1½ cups all-purpose flour	

Combine the eggs, milk, salt, sugar and lemon rind in a bowl. Stir in the flour and mix with a whisk or spoon until the ingredients are well combined. Heat a 7″ or 8″ skillet and grease lightly. Add 3 tablespoons of the batter and quickly tilt the pan to spread evenly. Cook over medium heat until the underside is golden. Turn over and cook on the other side. Keep warm in a preheated very slow (200°F.) oven. Continue to cook the others. Spread with jam or jelly and sprinkle with slivered almonds and confectioners' sugar. Roll up and arrange, folded sides underneath, side by side, in a buttered shallow baking dish. Spread the yogurt evenly over them. Bake, covered with foil, in a preheated moderate oven (350°F.) for 20 minutes. Makes about 14.

Jewish Yogurt Cheese Blintzes

Blintzes, or leaves, small filled pancakes, are highly esteemed Jewish culinary treasures and may be filled with various ingredients. This variation, made with yogurt, has a sweet cottage cheese filling.

1½ cups sifted all purpose flour
1 teaspoon salt
1 cup water
1 cup plain yogurt
5 eggs

Shortening for frying
1 pound cottage cheese
2 tablespoons sugar
1 teaspoon grated lemon rind

Combine the flour and salt in a large bowl. Pour in the water and mix until smooth. Add the yogurt and mix again. Beat 4 of the eggs and add to the mixture. Beat until smooth and thin. Heat a 7" or 8" skillet and grease lightly. Add 3 tablespoons of the batter all at once. Tilt the pan to spread evenly and cook over low heat until bubbles form on the surface. Turn to brown lightly on the other side. Turn out onto a dry surface and keep warm in a preheated very slow (200° F.) oven while cooking the others. Continue to cook the pancakes, greasing the pan as necessary. Combine the cottage cheese, sugar, lemon rind and remaining egg. Mix to thoroughly combine the ingredients. Place a tablespoon of filling on each pancake. Fold over the sides and roll up each one. Fry in shortening or butter until golden, being careful while turning so the filling does not come out. Serve with plain yogurt, if desired. Makes about 16.

Southern Yogurt Corn Muffins

The addition of yogurt to this old favorite results in light and flavorful muffins.

¾ cup yellow cornmeal	¾ teaspoon salt
1 cup all-purpose flour	1 cup plain yogurt
¼ cup sugar	1 egg, slightly beaten
1 teaspoon baking powder	2 tablespoons shortening,
1 teaspoon baking soda	melted

Combine the first six ingredients in a large bowl. Make a well in the center and add the remaining ingredients. Stir to blend them. Spoon into greased muffin tins, filling ⅔ full. Bake in a preheated hot (425°F.) oven for 25 minutes, or until cooked and golden. Makes 10 muffins.

Yogurt Gingerbread

Molasses, an important American sweetener since colonial times, is a popular health food and provides iron and calcium. It is used in making many baked goods including this well known favorite.

⅓ cup shortening or margarine, softened	2 teaspoons baking powder
	¼ teaspoon baking soda
½ cup sugar	1 teaspoon ground ginger
1 egg	1 teaspoon ground cinna-
⅔ cup light molasses	mon
⅔ cup plain yogurt	¼ teaspoon ground cloves
2 cups unsifted cake flour	½ teaspoon salt

Cream the shortening in a large bowl. Add the sugar and beat until light and fluffy. Add the egg and mix well.

Stir in the molasses and then the yogurt. Sift the flour, baking powder and soda, ginger, cinnamon, cloves and salt into the yogurt mixture and blend together the ingredients. Turn into a greased 9″ square pan and bake in a preheated moderate oven (350°F.) for about 40 minutes or until done. Cool 5 minutes before removing from the pan. Serve warm or cold with whipped cream or plain yogurt, if desired. Serves 8.

Honey Yogurt Coffeecake

Serve with any favorite beverage for a morning get together or as a brunch dessert.

1½ cups all-purpose flour
1 teaspoon baking powder
½ teaspoon baking soda
½ teaspoon salt
1 egg
1 cup plain yogurt

⅓ cup honey
3 tablespoons melted
    shortening
Honey-nut topping (recipe
    below)

Sift the flour, baking powder and soda and salt into a large bowl. Combine the egg, yogurt, honey and melted shortening and mix well. Stir into the sifted ingredients and mix well. Turn into a buttered 9″ square pan and cover with the honey topping. Bake in a preheated hot oven (400°F.) for about 30 minutes, or until done. Serves 8 to 10.

Honey Nut Topping

¼ cup butter or margarine
¼ cup sugar
4 tablespoons flour

¼ cup honey
¼ cup chopped nuts

Cream the butter. Stir in the sugar, flour and honey and mix well. Add the nuts.

Banana Yogurt Muffins with Wheat Germ

Another good quick bread made with the addition of wheat germ.

1½ cups unsifted all-purpose flour	½ teaspoon salt
½ cup wheat germ	1 cup mashed bananas
⅓ cup sugar	(about 2 large)
2 teaspoons baking powder	½ to ⅔ cup plain yogurt
1 teaspoon baking soda	¼ cup melted shortening
	1 large egg

Put the flour, wheat germ, sugar, baking powder, baking soda and salt in a large bowl and stir well. Combine the bananas, yogurt, shortening and egg in a small bowl and mix well with a fork. Add to the dry ingredients and mix to blend. Spoon into greased muffin tins, filling ⅔ full. Bake in a preheated hot (400°F.) oven for about 20 minutes, or until done. Makes 14.

Prune Yogurt Whip

This is an easy to prepare dessert made with flavored yogurt. Substitute any other favorite fruit flavor (blueberry, strawberry, peach) for the prune yogurt, if desired.

1 egg white	½ teaspoon fresh lemon
2 tablespoons sugar	juice
Dash salt	1 cup prune yogurt
	1 cup plain yogurt

Beat the egg white until stiff. Add the sugar and salt and beat again. Fold in the lemon juice and prune yogurt and chill. Serve with the plain yogurt spooned over it. Serves 4.

Yogurt Raisin Rice Pudding

A good family dessert.

2 cups cooked rice
1½ cups light cream or
    milk
1½ cups plain yogurt

½ cup honey
3 eggs, slightly beaten
1 cup chopped raisins

Combine the rice, cream, yogurt and honey. Mix in the eggs and then the raisins. Turn into a greased baking dish and cook in a preheated moderate (350°F.) oven for 1 hour, or until done. Serve with cream, if desired. Serves 8.

Orange Yogurt Chiffon Pie

A light cake or pie called chiffon is made with the addition of fluffy beaten egg whites.

1⅓ cups vanilla wafer
    crumbs
¼ cup butter or marga-
    rine, melted
2 tablespoons (2 enve-
    lopes) unflavored
    gelatin
10 tablespoons sugar

1 cup water
2 cups plain yogurt
1 can (6 ounces) frozen
    concentrated orange
    juice, thawed
2 egg whites
Toasted coconut

Combine the crumbs and butter in a bowl. Press the mixture firmly and evenly over the bottom and sides of a 9-inch pie plate. Chill. Combine the gelatin and ½ cup (8 tablespoons) of sugar in a medium saucepan. Add the water and heat over low heat, stirring, until the gelatin is dissolved. Remove from the heat. Combine the yogurt and orange juice in a bowl and stir in the gelatin mixture. Chill until partially set. Beat the egg whites until frothy. Add the remaining 2 tablespoons of sugar and beat until stiff. Fold into the orange mixture and chill until it begins to set. Spoon into the crust and chill until set. Garnish with toasted coconut. Serves 6.

Yogurt Date Fruit Cookies

The fruit of the date palm is one of our oldest and most treasured foods which provides goodness and flavor to many interesting desserts.

½ cup butter or margarine	½ teaspoon salt
1 cup firmly packed light brown sugar	½ teaspoon baking soda
	½ cup plain yogurt
1 egg	½ cup chopped dates
2 cups all-purpose flour	⅔ cup candied diced fruit
2 teaspoons baking powder	

Cream the butter in a large bowl and mix in the sugar. Beat until light and creamy. Add the egg. Sift the flour, baking powder, salt and soda into the mixture, adding alternately with the yogurt. Stir to blend the ingredients and mix in the dates and fruit. Drop by well filled teaspoonfuls onto lightly greased cookie sheets and bake in a preheated hot (400°F.) oven for 12 to 15 minutes. Makes about 3 dozen.

Mixed Fruit Ambrosia

This is a good summer dessert for an outdoor or indoor meal.

3 medium oranges, peeled and sliced	2 tablespoons honey
8 slices canned pineapple	1 tablespoon lemon juice
2 medium bananas, peeled and sliced	1 cup plain yogurt
3 cups sliced fresh or frozen strawberries	1 can (3½ ounces) flaked coconut

Arrange the fruit in a bowl. Combine the honey and lemon juice and spoon over the fruit. Toss lightly. Chill.

When ready to serve add the yogurt and toss the fruit. Sprinkle with the coconut. Serves 6 to 8.

Yogurt Bread Pudding

Another early American favorite is enhanced with the addition of yogurt.

1 cup hot milk	½ cup honey
1 cup plain yogurt	2 eggs, well beaten
3 tablespoons melted butter or margarine	½ teaspoon ground cinnamon
3 cups white or whole-wheat bread cubes, crusts removed	1 teaspoon vanilla
	Dash salt
	½ cup seedless raisins

Combine the milk, yogurt and butter in a large bowl and add the bread cubes and honey. When cool stir in the remaining ingredients and spoon into a buttered baking dish. Cook in a preheated medium oven (350°F.) for 1 hour, or until done. Serves 6. Serve with cream, if desired.

Lime Yogurt Pie

Limes are the fruit of tropical trees which are grown in this country in California and Florida. The citrus fruit is a good source of vitamin C and is used in making many delectable desserts such as this pie.

1⅓ cups graham cracker crumbs	1 cup boiling water
2 tablespoons sugar	1 package (8 ounces) cream cheese
¼ cup butter, melted	1 cup plain yogurt
1 package (3 ounces) lime flavor gelatin	Grated semi-sweet chocolate

Combine the crumbs and sugar in a small bowl and stir in the butter. Press the mixture firmly and evenly on the bottom and sides of a 9-inch pie plate. Chill. Put the gelatin in a small bowl and pour the water over it. Stir until dissolved. In a small bowl beat the cheese until fluffy. Add slowly the dissolved gelatin and chill until partially set. Fold in the yogurt and turn into the crust. Chill. Garnish with the grated chocolate. Serves 6.

Easy Yogurt Fruit Sherbet

Put 1 cup of yogurt in a freezing tray and freeze until mushy. Take out of the tray and mix with 1 cup crushed pineapple, including the liquid. Return to the freezing compartment and leave until a soft mush. Remove and beat well. Return to the tray and freeze until solid. Serves 4.
Note: This may be made also with sweetened mashed strawberries or raspberries.

Yogurt Apple Pie

The all-American favorite, apple pie, has yet one more variation with the addition of yogurt.

1 cup firmly packed light brown sugar	*Standard pastry for double-crust 8 or 9 inch pie*
½ teaspoon ground cinnamon	*6 tart apples, cored, pared and sliced*
1 tablespoon flour	*½ cup plain yogurt*
¼ teaspoon salt	

Combine the sugar, cinnamon, flour and salt and set aside. Fit one half of the rolled out pie pastry into the pan and trim off any surplus pastry. Arrange the apple slices over the pastry. Sprinkle with the sugar mixture and spoon the yogurt over the ingredients. Put the top pastry over the ingredients. Seal and flute the edges and cut slits in the pastry. Bake in a preheated hot (400°F.) oven for 10 minutes. Lower the heat to 375°F. and cook about 30 minutes longer, or until done. Cool slightly before serving. Serves 6.

Blueberry Yogurt Cream Puffs

An easy-to-prepare party dessert.

2 cups heavy or whipping cream
1/4 cup sugar
1/4 teaspoon salt
1/2 teaspoon vanilla
2 cups blueberry yogurt
24 medium cream puffs
Confectioners' sugar

Combine the cream, sugar, salt and vanilla in a bowl and whip until stiff. Fold in the yogurt and spoon into the puffs. Chill. Serve sprinkled with confectioners' sugar. Serves 12.

Yogurt Ice Cream Dishes

Banana Split

For 1 portion split 1 peeled ripe banana in half lengthwise. Arrange in a dish. Place 1 scoop of chocolate and 1 of strawberry ice cream over the banana. Top with 1/2 cup of plain or fruit-flavored yogurt and sprinkle with chopped nuts. Top with whipped cream, if desired.

Parfait

Alternate layers of vanilla ice cream and thawed frozen strawberries, strawberry or plain yogurt and chopped nuts in a parfait glass. Top with whipped cream and a maraschino cherry.

Peach Sundae

Top peach or vanilla ice cream with sweetened sliced fresh or canned peaches, yogurt and chocolate sprinkles.

Melon à la Mode

Fill a chilled cantaloupe half with a scoop of ice cream and top with a mixture of plain yogurt. berries and sugar.

Apricot Pineapple Cup

Apricots, one of our most attractive fruits, are rich in vitamin A and are good either fresh, canned or dried.

1 can (1 pound) whole peeled apricots, drained
1½ cups drained canned pineapple chunks

2 teaspoons fresh lemon juice
2 tablespoons honey
1 cup plain yogurt
Fresh mint leaves

Spoon the fruit into a bowl. Combine the lemon juice, honey and yogurt and add to the fruit. Toss lightly and chill. Serve in dessert dishes garnished with mint leaves. Serves 4.

Cream Cheese Yogurt Pie

This dessert can be quickly and easily prepared for an impromptu occasion.

1 cup plain yogurt
½ pound cream cheese, softened
1 tablespoon honey
¼ teaspoon vanilla

½ cup drained crushed pineapple
1 single 8 inch baked pie crust

Combine the first five ingredients and mix well. Spoon into the pie crust and chill. Serves 6.

Yogurt Strawberry Shortcake

During the fresh strawberry season everybody likes to enjoy this classic American preparation. It can also be made with frozen strawberries when the fruit is out of season.

1½ cups all-purpose flour
2 tablespoons sugar
2 teaspoons baking powder
¼ teaspoon baking soda
¼ teaspoon salt

¼ cup butter or margarine
¾ cup plain yogurt
1 quart strawberries, sliced and sweetened
Sweetened whipped cream

Sift the flour, sugar, baking powder, soda and salt into a bowl. Cut in the butter and then add the yogurt. Stir to combine the ingredients. Roll out on a floured surface to ½-inch thickness. Cut into 3-inch biscuits with a biscuit cutter. Place on a baking sheet and bake in a preheated hot oven (450°F.) about 12 minutes, or until done. Split in halves and spoon the strawberries in the middle and on top. Spoon whipped cream over them. Serves 6.

Yogurt Oatmeal Cookies

One of the best ways of utilizing nutritious oats is in the preparation of cookies. These are good snacks.

¾ cup softened butter or margarine	½ cup plain yogurt
1 cup dark or light brown sugar	1 teaspoon vanilla
	1 cup all-purpose flour
½ cup white sugar	1 teaspoon salt
1 egg	½ teaspoon baking soda
	3 cups oats

Cream the butter in a large bowl and mix in the sugars. Beat well. Add the egg and then the yogurt and vanilla, beating after each addition. Sift the flour, salt and soda into the mixture and stir well. Mix in the oats. Drop by heaping teaspoonfuls onto greased cookie sheets. Bake in a preheated moderate oven (350°F.) for about 12 minutes, or until done. Makes about 4½ dozen.

Balkan Yogurt Cake

This is a traditional dessert enjoyed in the Balkans and some Middle Eastern countries.

½ cup butter or margarine	2 teaspoons grated lemon rind
⅔ cup sugar	
2 eggs	1 cup plain yogurt

2 cups sifted all-purpose
    flour
2 teaspoons baking powder

½ teaspoon baking soda
½ teaspoon salt
Confectioners' sugar

Cream the butter in a large bowl. Add the sugar and beat with a spoon or electric mixer until creamy and light. Add the eggs, one at a time, beating after each addition. Stir in the lemon rind and yogurt and beat again. Sift the flour, baking powder and soda and salt into the yogurt mixture and beat until smooth. Turn into a greased 9-inch square pan and bake in a preheated moderate oven (350°F.) for about 35 minutes, or until done. Cool for 5 minutes. Turn out on a rack and cool. Sprinkle with confectioners' sugar and serve while still warm. Serves about 10.

Russian Buckwheat Blini

Small, thin buckwheat pancakes called *blini* or *bleeny*, eaten as appetizers, are traditionally served with melted butter, smoked fish or caviar and sour cream. They are also good when topped with yogurt and served as a supper entrée.

1 package active dry yeast
    or 1 cake yeast
1 cup lukewarm water
1 cup lukewarm milk
1¼ cups lukewarm plain
    yogurt
¼ cup butter, melted

1 egg, slightly beaten
1 cup all-purpose flour
2 cups buckwheat flour
1 teaspoon salt
1 teaspoon sugar
Butter or margarine for fry-
    ing

Sprinkle the yeast or crumble the cake in a large bowl. Add the lukewarm water (slightly warmer for the dry yeast) and after a minute or two, stir to dissolve. Mix together the milk, yogurt, butter and egg and add to the yeast mixture. Add the flours, salt and sugar, stirring after each addition. Beat well. Cover the bowl with a light towel and leave in a warm place until doubled in bulk, about 2 hours. Beat well.

To cook, drop by large tablespoonsful onto a lightly greased hot griddle or frying pan, if needed. Keep in a preheated very slow (200°F.) oven while frying the others. Each *blini* should be about 3″ in diameter. To serve, pile high on a warm platter. Spread with melted butter and top with a small spoonful of yogurt and a garnish of smoked fish or caviar. Serves 8 to 10.

Breakfast Yogurt Pancakes

Prepare these pancakes beforehand and keep refrigerated to use for breakfast.

2 cups plain yogurt	½ teaspoon baking soda
½ cup milk	½ teaspoon salt
2 eggs, slightly beaten	2 tablespoons melted butter or margarine
2 cups all-purpose flour	
2 teaspoons sugar	Fat for frying
1 teaspoon baking powder	

Combine all the ingredients, except the fat, in a bowl, and stir together until well mixed. Pour 3 tablespoons of the batter onto a hot greased griddle or frying pan. When bubbles form on the top turn over and cook on the other side. Keep warm in a preheated very slow (200°F.) oven while frying the others. Serve with butter and maple syrup. Serves 6 to 8.

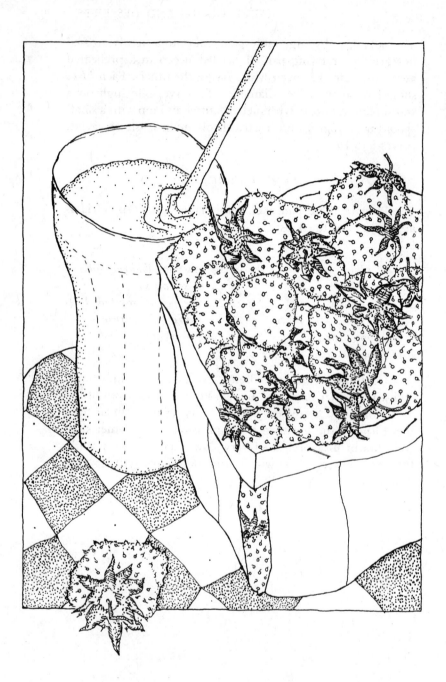

Beverages

Beverages made with yogurt have great appeal as they can be easily and quickly prepared, and have versatile roles in our menus and diet.

Many of the drinks, called variously floats, cobblers, nogs, shakes, frappés or sodas, among others, can simply be mixed in an electric blender, a large glass or a covered container. Generally they are made with a few ingredients which are kitchen staples for the most part.

Yogurt beverages may be served for breakfast, as pre-meal drinks, appetizers and desserts, or as snacks. They are appealing to children as well as adults. Some are low in calories while others are not particularly designed for weight-watchers. All, however, are nourishing and appealing.

Given below are a number of representative selections.

Tomato Yogurt Appetizer

A good luncheon or dinner first course or pre-meal beverage.

4 cups tomato juice
1 cup plain yogurt
1 teaspoon lemon juice
½ teaspoon dried basil

2 or 3 drops tabasco
2 tablespoons chopped
    fresh parsley
Salt, pepper to taste

Combine the ingredients and mix well. Chill. Serves 4 to 6.

Vanilla Yogurt Milkshake

A nourishing snack.

1 cup chilled milk
½ cup chilled plain yogurt
1 to 2 teaspoons sugar

⅛ teaspoon vanilla extract
½ to ¾ cup vanilla ice
    cream

Whirl the ingredients in a blender or mix well. Pour into glasses. Serves 2.

Banana Yogurt Frosted

An appealing summer beverage.

4 ripe bananas, peeled and
    mashed
2 cups chilled milk

2 cups chilled plain yogurt
1 cup vanilla ice cream
Dash grated nutmeg

Whirl the ingredients in a blender or mix well. Serve in chilled glasses. Serves 6 to 8.

Yogurt Malted Milk

An old favorite has additional appeal with the addition of yogurt.

1 cup fresh milk
1¼ tablespoons malted
    milk
2 teaspoons honey

½ cup plain yogurt
½ cup ice cream (vanilla,
    chocolate or any fla-
    vor)

Combine the ingredients and mix well. Chill. Serves 2.

Fresh Strawberry Yogurt Cooler

A refreshing drink to make with fresh strawberries.

1 pint fresh strawberries   2 cups plain yogurt
3 tablespoons honey

Clean the strawberries. Purée them and mix with the honey and yogurt. Chill. Serves 4.

Pineapple Yogurt Float

Children will enjoy this float for a dessert or snack.

2 cups chilled pineapple   ¼ cup powdered milk
    juice   ½ cup pineapple sherbet
2 cups chilled plain yogurt   or vanilla ice cream

Combine the first three ingredients to mix well. Pour into 2 chilled large glasses. Put ¼ cup of sherbet or ice cream into each. Serves 2.

Prune Yogurt Cooler

A refreshing warm-weather beverage.

2 cups chilled prune juice   ¼ teaspoon ground cinna-
2 cups chilled plain yogurt   mon or nutmeg
2 teaspoons fresh lemon
    juice

Blend together the ingredients to mix well. Serves 4.

Nourishing Yogurt Drink

Wheat germ, honey and molasses add flavor and nutrients to this drink.

2 cups plain yogurt   2 tablespoons wheat germ
2 cups fresh milk   1 tablespoon honey
½ cup powdered milk   1 tablespoon molasses

Combine the ingredients and chill. Serves 4.

Maple Yogurt Ice Cream Soda

A good dessert or in-between-meal snack.

8 tablespoons maple syrup   4 scoops vanilla ice cream
1 cup chilled plain yogurt   Chilled soda water

Put 2 tablespoons of maple syrup in each of 4 tall glasses. Stir ¼ cup of yogurt into each one and add a scoop of ice cream. Fill the glass with soda and stir. Serves 4.

Iced Chocolate Yogurt Drink

An inviting beverage-dessert for a ladies' luncheon.

2 cups chilled milk   Dash grated nutmeg
2 cups chilled plain yogurt   Whipped cream
½ cup chocolate syrup

Combine the milk, yogurt and syrup and blend well. Serve in tall glasses topped with whipped cream and nutmeg. Serves 3 to 4.

Apricot Orange Nog

A good breakfast or snack beverage.

2 cups fresh or frozen   1 cup plain yogurt
     orange juice   Fresh mint leaves
1 cup apricot juice

Combine the first three ingredients and chill. Serve in glasses garnished with mint leaves. Serves 4.

Yogurt Lemon Apple Drink

An interesting beverage for a mid-afternoon break.

1 can (6 ounces) frozen
   lemonade concentrate

4 cups chilled apple juice
2 cups chilled plain yogurt

Combine the lemonade concentrate and apple juice to mix well. Add the yogurt and mix again. Serves 6.

Mocha Yogurt Shake

A rich and flavorful ice cream drink.

2 tablespoons instant coffee
   powder
½ cup chocolate syrup
1 scoop coffee ice cream

1 scoop chocolate ice cream
1½ cups chilled milk
1½ cups chilled plain
   yogurt

Combine the ingredients in a large blender or mix well. Serves 4 to 6.

Cranberry Yogurt Cooler

Serve for a summer ladies' luncheon or tea.

2 cups chilled cranberry
   juice

2 cups chilled ginger ale
2 cups chilled plain yogurt

Combine the cranberry juice and yogurt to mix well. Add the ginger ale and mix again. Serves 4 to 6.

Party Yogurt Eggnog

6 eggs
¾ cup sugar
1 pint chilled light cream
1 cup chilled milk

1 cup chilled plain yogurt
2 cups bourbon whiskey
Grated nutmeg

Separate the eggs and mix the yolks with the sugar. Beat well. Gradually add the cream and milk and then the yogurt and whiskey. Beat well. Chill. Beat the egg whites until stiff and fold into the mixture. Sprinkle with nutmeg. Makes about 20 servings.

Breakfast Yogurt Eggnog

An easy-to-prepare and nourishing breakfast drink.

2 eggs, separated	1 cup chilled plain yogurt
1 to 2 tablespoons sugar	½ teaspoon vanilla extract
1 cup chilled fresh milk	Grated nutmeg

Mix the egg yolks until light and creamy. Stir in the sugar, milk, yogurt and vanilla. Beat the egg whites until stiff and fold into the mixture. Serve garnished with the nutmeg. Serves 4.

Tomato Yogurt Pick-up

A low calorie snack beverage.

½ cup chilled tomato juice	2 tablespoons chopped fresh parsley
½ cup chilled plain yogurt	1 teaspoon fresh lemon juice

Combine the ingredients to mix well. Serves 1.

Winter Yogurt Hot Cocoa

A good drink to serve as a winter snack.

6 tablespoons cocoa	2½ cups fresh milk
6 tablespoons sugar	2½ cups plain yogurt
⅛ teaspoon salt	½ teaspoon vanilla extract
½ cup water	

Combine the cocoa, sugar and salt in a saucepan and add the water. Heat over a low fire until well mixed. Add the milk and heat slowly, stirring, and then add the yogurt. Leave on the stove until heated through, beating until frothy. Add the vanilla. Top with a marshmallow or whipped cream, if desired. Serves 6 to 8.

Turkish Yogurt Ayran

A traditional summer drink in Turkey and also other Near Eastern countries is made by diluting yogurt with an equal quantity of water. It is seasoned with a pinch of salt.

Yogurt Iced Coffee Frappé

Serve as a nourishing breakfast or mid-afternoon drink.

2 eggs, beaten	1 cup plain yogurt
½ cup sugar	½ cup heavy cream,
3 cups strong coffee	whipped

Combine the eggs, sugar, coffee and yogurt and mix well. Serve topped with the whipped cream. Serves 4.

Recipe Index

BASIC YOGURT RECIPES 21

BEVERAGES 207

A CATALOGUE OF SELECTED DOVER BOOKS
IN ALL FIELDS OF INTEREST

A CATALOGUE OF SELECTED DOVER BOOKS
IN ALL FIELDS OF INTEREST

THE DEVIL'S DICTIONARY, Ambrose Bierce. Barbed, bitter, brilliant witticisms in the form of a dictionary. Best, most ferocious satire America has produced. 145pp. 20487-1 Pa. $1.75

ABSOLUTELY MAD INVENTIONS, A.E. Brown, H.A. Jeffcott. Hilarious, useless, or merely absurd inventions all granted patents by the U.S. Patent Office. Edible tie pin, mechanical hat tipper, etc. 57 illustrations. 125pp. 22596-8 Pa. $1.50

AMERICAN WILD FLOWERS COLORING BOOK, Paul Kennedy. Planned coverage of 48 most important wildflowers, from Rickett's collection; instructive as well as entertaining. Color versions on covers. 48pp. 8¼ x 11. 20095-7 Pa. $1.50

BIRDS OF AMERICA COLORING BOOK, John James Audubon. Rendered for coloring by Paul Kennedy. 46 of Audubon's noted illustrations: red-winged blackbird, cardinal, purple finch, towhee, etc. Original plates reproduced in full color on the covers. 48pp. 8¼ x 11. 23049-X Pa. $1.35

NORTH AMERICAN INDIAN DESIGN COLORING BOOK, Paul Kennedy. The finest examples from Indian masks, beadwork, pottery, etc. — selected and redrawn for coloring (with identifications) by well-known illustrator Paul Kennedy. 48pp. 8¼ x 11. 21125-8 Pa. $1.35

UNIFORMS OF THE AMERICAN REVOLUTION COLORING BOOK, Peter Copeland. 31 lively drawings reproduce whole panorama of military attire; each uniform has complete instructions for accurate coloring. (Not in the Pictorial Archives Series). 64pp. 8¼ x 11. 21850-3 Pa. $1.50

THE WONDERFUL WIZARD OF OZ COLORING BOOK, L. Frank Baum. Color the Yellow Brick Road and much more in 61 drawings adapted from W.W. Denslow's originals, accompanied by abridged version of text. Dorothy, Toto, Oz and the Emerald City. 61 illustrations. 64pp. 8¼ x 11. 20452-9 Pa. $1.50

CUT AND COLOR PAPER MASKS, Michael Grater. Clowns, animals, funny faces... simply color them in, cut them out, and put them together, and you have 9 paper masks to play with and enjoy. Complete instructions. Assembled masks shown in full color on the covers. 32pp. 8¼ x 11. 23171-2 Pa. $1.50

STAINED GLASS CHRISTMAS ORNAMENT COLORING BOOK, Carol Belanger Grafton. Brighten your Christmas season with over 100 Christmas ornaments done in a stained glass effect on translucent paper. Color them in and then hang at windows, from lights, anywhere. 32pp. 8¼ x 11. 20707-2 Pa. $1.75

THE ART DECO STYLE, ed. by Theodore Menten. Furniture, jewelry, metalwork, ceramics, fabrics, lighting fixtures, interior decors, exteriors, graphics from pure French sources. Best sampling around. Over 400 photographs. 183pp. 8⅜ x 11¼.
22824-X Pa. $4.00

THE GENTLEMAN AND CABINET MAKER'S DIRECTOR, Thomas Chippendale. Full reprint, 1762 style book, most influential of all time; chairs, tables, sofas, mirrors, cabinets, etc. 200 plates, plus 24 photographs of surviving pieces. 249pp. 9⅞ x 12¾.
21601-2 Pa. $5.00

PINE FURNITURE OF EARLY NEW ENGLAND, Russell H. Kettell. Basic book. Thorough historical text, plus 200 illustrations of boxes, highboys, candlesticks, desks, etc. 477pp. 7⅞ x 10¾.
20145-7 Clothbd. $12.50

ORIENTAL RUGS, ANTIQUE AND MODERN, Walter A. Hawley. Persia, Turkey, Caucasus, Central Asia, China, other traditions. Best general survey of all aspects: styles and periods, manufacture, uses, symbols and their interpretation, and identification. 96 illustrations, 11 in color. 320pp. 6⅛ x 9¼.
22366-3 Pa. $5.00

DECORATIVE ANTIQUE IRONWORK, Henry R. d'Allemagne. Photographs of 4500 iron artifacts from world's finest collection, Rouen. Hinges, locks, candelabra, weapons, lighting devices, clocks, tools, from Roman times to mid-19th century. Nothing else comparable to it. 420pp. 9 x 12.
22082-6 Pa. $8.50

THE COMPLETE BOOK OF DOLL MAKING AND COLLECTING, Catherine Christopher. Instructions, patterns for dozens of dolls, from rag doll on up to elaborate, historically accurate figures. Mould faces, sew clothing, make doll houses, etc. Also collecting information. Many illustrations. 288pp. 6 x 9. 22066-4 Pa. $3.00

ANTIQUE PAPER DOLLS: 1915-1920, edited by Arnold Arnold. 7 antique cut-out dolls and 24 costumes from 1915-1920, selected by Arnold Arnold from his collection of rare children's books and entertainments, all in full color. 32pp. 9¼ x 12¼.
23176-3 Pa. $2.00

ANTIQUE PAPER DOLLS: THE EDWARDIAN ERA, Epinal. Full-color reproductions of two historic series of paper dolls that show clothing styles in 1908 and at the beginning of the First World War. 8 two-sided, stand-up dolls and 32 complete, two-sided costumes. Full instructions for assembling included. 32pp. 9¼ x 12¼.
23175-5 Pa. $2.00

A HISTORY OF COSTUME, Carl Köhler, Emma von Sichardt. Egypt, Babylon, Greece up through 19th century Europe; based on surviving pieces, art works, etc. Full text and 595 illustrations, including many clear, measured patterns for reproducing historic costume. Practical. 464pp.
21030-8 Pa. $4.00

EARLY AMERICAN LOCOMOTIVES, John H. White, Jr. Finest locomotive engravings from late 19th century: historical (1804-1874), main-line (after 1870), special, foreign, etc. 147 plates. 200pp. 11⅜ x 8¼.
22772-3 Pa. $3.50

VICTORIAN HOUSES: A TREASURY OF LESSER-KNOWN EXAMPLES, Edmund Gillon and Clay Lancaster. 116 photographs, excellent commentary illustrate distinct characteristics, many borrowings of local Victorian architecture. Octagonal houses, Americanized chalets, grand country estates, small cottages, etc. Rich heritage often overlooked. 116 plates. 11⅜ x 10.   22966-1 Pa. $4.00

STICKS AND STONES, Lewis Mumford. Great classic of American cultural history; architecture from medieval-inspired earliest forms to 20th century; evolution of structure and style, influence of environment. 21 illustrations. 113pp.
20202-X Pa. $2.00

ON THE LAWS OF JAPANESE PAINTING, Henry P. Bowie. Best substitute for training with genius Oriental master, based on years of study in Kano school. Philosophy, brushes, inks, style, etc. 66 illustrations. 117pp. 6⅛ x 9¼.   20030-2 Pa. $4.00

A HANDBOOK OF ANATOMY FOR ART STUDENTS, Arthur Thomson. Virtually exhaustive. Skeletal structure, muscles, heads, special features. Full text, anatomical figures, undraped photos. Male and female. 337 illustrations. 459pp.
21163-0 Pa. $5.00

AN ATLAS OF ANATOMY FOR ARTISTS, Fritz Schider. Finest text, working book. Full text, plus anatomical illustrations; plates by great artists showing anatomy. 593 illustrations. 192pp. 7⅞ x 10¾.   20241-0 Clothbd. $6.95

THE HUMAN FIGURE IN MOTION, Eadweard Muybridge. More than 4500 stopped-action photos, in action series, showing undraped men, women, children jumping, lying down, throwing, sitting, wrestling, carrying, etc. "Unparalleled dictionary for artists," American Artist. Taken by great 19th century photographer. 390pp. 7⅞ x 10⅝.   20204-6 Clothbd. $12.50

AN ATLAS OF ANIMAL ANATOMY FOR ARTISTS, W. Ellenberger et al. Horses, dogs, cats, lions, cattle, deer, etc. Muscles, skeleton, surface features. The basic work. Enlarged edition. 288 illustrations. 151pp. 9⅜ x 12¼.   20082-5 Pa. $4.00

LETTER FORMS: 110 COMPLETE ALPHABETS, Frederick Lambert. 110 sets of capital letters; 16 lower case alphabets; 70 sets of numbers and other symbols. Edited and expanded by Theodore Menten. 110pp. 8⅛ x 11.   22872-X Pa. $2.50

THE METHODS OF CONSTRUCTION OF CELTIC ART, George Bain. Simple geometric techniques for making wonderful Celtic interlacements, spirals, Kells-type initials, animals, humans, etc. Unique for artists, craftsmen. Over 500 illustrations. 160pp. 9 x 12.   USO 22923-8 Pa. $4.00

SCULPTURE, PRINCIPLES AND PRACTICE, Louis Slobodkin. Step by step approach to clay, plaster, metals, stone; classical and modern. 253 drawings, photos. 255pp. 8⅛ x 11.   22960-2 Pa. $4.50

THE ART OF ETCHING, E.S. Lumsden. Clear, detailed instructions for etching, drypoint, softground, aquatint; from 1st sketch to print. Very detailed, thorough. 200 illustrations. 376pp.   20049-3 Pa. $3.50

JEWISH GREETING CARDS, Ed Sibbett, Jr. 16 cards to cut and color. Three say "Happy Chanukah," one "Happy New Year," others have no message, show stars of David, Torahs, wine cups, other traditional themes. 16 envelopes. 8¼ x 11.
23225-5 Pa. $2.00

AUBREY BEARDSLEY GREETING CARD BOOK, Aubrey Beardsley. Edited by Theodore Menten. 16 elegant yet inexpensive greeting cards let you combine your own sentiments with subtle Art Nouveau lines. 16 different Aubrey Beardsley designs that you can color or not, as you wish. 16 envelopes. 64pp. 8¼ x 11.
23173-9 Pa. $2.00

RECREATIONS IN THE THEORY OF NUMBERS, Albert Beiler. Number theory, an inexhaustible source of puzzles, recreations, for beginners and advanced. Divisors, perfect numbers. scales of notation, etc. 349pp. 21096-0 Pa. $2.50

AMUSEMENTS IN MATHEMATICS, Henry E. Dudeney. One of largest puzzle collections, based on algebra, arithmetic, permutations, probability, plane figure dissection, properties of numbers, by one of world's foremost puzzlists. Solutions. 450 illustrations. 258pp. 20473-1 Pa. $2.75

MATHEMATICS, MAGIC AND MYSTERY, Martin Gardner. Puzzle editor for Scientific American explains math behind: card tricks, stage mind reading, coin and match tricks, counting out games, geometric dissections. Probability, sets, theory of numbers, clearly explained. Plus more than 400 tricks, guaranteed to work. 135 illustrations. 176pp. 20335-2 Pa. $2.00

BEST MATHEMATICAL PUZZLES OF SAM LOYD, edited by Martin Gardner. Bizarre, original, whimsical puzzles by America's greatest puzzler. From fabulously rare Cyclopedia, including famous 14-15 puzzles, the Horse of a Different Color, 115 more. Elementary math. 150 illustrations. 167pp. 20498-7 Pa. $2.00

MATHEMATICAL PUZZLES FOR BEGINNERS AND ENTHUSIASTS, Geoffrey Mott-Smith. 189 puzzles from easy to difficult involving arithmetic, logic, algebra, properties of digits, probability. Explanation of math behind puzzles. 135 illustrations. 248pp. 20198-8 Pa. $2.75 ·

BIG BOOK OF MAZES AND LABYRINTHS, Walter Shepherd. Classical, solid, and ripple mazes; short path and avoidance labyrinths; more — 50 mazes and labyrinths in all. 12 other figures. Full solutions. 112pp. 8⅛ x 11. 22951-3 Pa. $2.00

COIN GAMES AND PUZZLES, Maxey Brooke. 60 puzzles, games and stunts — from Japan, Korea, Africa and the ancient world, by Dudeney and the other great puzzlers, as well as Maxey Brooke's own creations. Full solutions. 67 illustrations. 94pp. 22893-2 Pa. $1.25

HAND SHADOWS TO BE THROWN UPON THE WALL, Henry Bursill. Wonderful Victorian novelty tells how to make flying birds, dog, goose, deer, and 14 others. 32pp. 6½ x 9¼. 21779-5 Pa. $1.25

DECORATIVE ALPHABETS AND INITIALS, edited by Alexander Nesbitt. 91 complete alphabets (medieval to modern), 3924 decorative initials, including Victorian novelty and Art Nouveau. 192pp. 7¾ x 10¾. 20544-4 Pa. $3.50

CALLIGRAPHY, Arthur Baker. Over 100 original alphabets from the hand of our greatest living calligrapher: simple, bold, fine-line, richly ornamented, etc. — all strikingly original and different, a fusion of many influences and styles. 155pp. 11⅜ x 8¼. 22895-9 Pa. $4.00

MONOGRAMS AND ALPHABETIC DEVICES, edited by Hayward and Blanche Cirker. Over 2500 combinations, names, crests in very varied styles: script engraving, ornate Victorian, simple Roman, and many others. 226pp. 8⅛ x 11. 22330-2 Pa. $5.00

THE BOOK OF SIGNS, Rudolf Koch. Famed German type designer renders 493 symbols: religious, alchemical, imperial, runes, property marks, etc. Timeless. 104pp. 6⅛ x 9¼. 20162-7 Pa. $1.50

200 DECORATIVE TITLE PAGES, edited by Alexander Nesbitt. 1478 to late 1920's. Baskerville, Dürer, Beardsley, W. Morris, Pyle, many others in most varied techniques. For posters, programs, other uses. 222pp. 8⅜ x 11¼. 21264-5 Pa. $3.50

DICTIONARY OF AMERICAN PORTRAITS, edited by Hayward and Blanche Cirker. 4000 important Americans, earliest times to 1905, mostly in clear line. Politicians, writers, soldiers, scientists, inventors, industrialists, Indians, Blacks, women, outlaws, etc. Identificatory information. 756pp. 9¼ x 12¾. 21823-6 Clothbd. $30.00

ART FORMS IN NATURE, Ernst Haeckel. Multitude of strangely beautiful natural forms: Radiolaria, Foraminifera, jellyfishes, fungi, turtles, bats, etc. All 100 plates of the 19th century evolutionist's Kunstformen der Natur (1904). 100pp. 9⅜ x 12¼. 22987-4 Pa. $4.00

DECOUPAGE: THE BIG PICTURE SOURCEBOOK, Eleanor Rawlings. Make hundreds of beautiful objects, over 550 florals, animals, letters, shells, period costumes, frames, etc. selected by foremost practitioner. Printed on one side of page. 8 color plates. Instructions. 176pp. 9³⁄₁₆ x 12¼. 23182-8 Pa. $5.00

AMERICAN FOLK DECORATION, Jean Lipman, Eve Meulendyke. Thorough coverage of all aspects of wood, tin, leather, paper, cloth decoration — scapes, humans, trees, flowers, geometrics — and how to make them. Full instructions. 233 illustrations, 5 in color. 163pp. 8⅜ x 11¼. 22217-9 Pa. $3.95

WHITTLING AND WOODCARVING, E.J. Tangerman. Best book on market; clear, full. If you can cut a potato, you can carve toys, puzzles, chains, caricatures, masks, patterns, frames, decorate surfaces, etc. Also covers serious wood sculpture. Over 200 photos. 293pp. 20965-2 Pa. $2.50

THE JOURNAL OF HENRY D. THOREAU, edited by Bradford Torrey, F.H. Allen. Complete reprinting of 14 volumes, 1837-1861, over two million words; the sourcebooks for Walden, etc. Definitive. All original sketches, plus 75 photographs. Introduction by Walter Harding. Total of 1804pp. 8½ x 12¼.
20312-3, 20313-1 Clothbd., Two vol. set $50.00

MASTERS OF THE DRAMA, John Gassner. Most comprehensive history of the drama, every tradition from Greeks to modern Europe and America, including Orient. Covers 800 dramatists, 2000 plays; biography, plot summaries, criticism, theatre history, etc. 77 illustrations. 890pp.
20100-7 Clothbd. $10.00

GHOST AND HORROR STORIES OF AMBROSE BIERCE, Ambrose Bierce. 23 modern horror stories: The Eyes of the Panther, The Damned Thing, etc., plus the dream-essay Visions of the Night. Edited by E.F. Bleiler. 199pp.
20767-6 Pa. $2.00

BEST GHOST STORIES, Algernon Blackwood. 13 great stories by foremost British 20th century supernaturalist. The Willows, The Wendigo, Ancient Sorceries, others. Edited by E.F. Bleiler. 366pp.
USO 22977-7 Pa. $3.00

THE BEST TALES OF HOFFMANN, E.T.A. Hoffmann. 10 of Hoffmann's most important stories, in modern re-editings of standard translations: Nutcracker and the King of Mice, The Golden Flowerpot, etc. 7 illustrations by Hoffmann. Edited by E.F. Bleiler. 458pp.
21793-0 Pa. $3.95

BEST GHOST STORIES OF J.S. LEFANU, J. Sheridan LeFanu. 16 stories by greatest Victorian master: Green Tea, Carmilla, Haunted Baronet, The Familiar, etc. Mostly unavailable elsewhere. Edited by E.F. Bleiler. 8 illustrations. 467pp.
20415-4 Pa. $4.00

SUPERNATURAL HORROR IN LITERATURE, H.P. Lovecraft. Great modern American supernaturalist brilliantly surveys history of genre to 1930's, summarizing, evaluating scores of books. Necessary for every student, lover of form. Introduction by E.F. Bleiler. 111pp.
20105-8 Pa. $1.50

THREE GOTHIC NOVELS, ed. by E.F. Bleiler. Full texts Castle of Otranto, Walpole; Vathek, Beckford; The Vampyre, Polidori; Fragment of a Novel, Lord Byron. 331pp.
21232-7 Pa. $3.00

SEVEN SCIENCE FICTION NOVELS, H.G. Wells. Full novels. First Men in the Moon, Island of Dr. Moreau, War of the Worlds, Food of the Gods, Invisible Man, Time Machine, In the Days of the Comet. A basic science-fiction library. 1015pp.
USO 20264-X Clothbd. $6.00

LADY AUDLEY'S SECRET, Mary E. Braddon. Great Victorian mystery classic, beautifully plotted, suspenseful; praised by Thackeray, Boucher, Starrett, others. What happened to beautiful, vicious Lady Audley's husband? Introduction by Norman Donaldson. 286pp.
23011-2 Pa. $3.00

CATALOGUE OF DOVER BOOKS

SLEEPING BEAUTY, illustrated by Arthur Rackham. Perhaps the fullest, most delightful version ever, told by C.S. Evans. Rackham's best work. 49 illustrations. 110pp. 7⅞ x 10¾.   22756-1 Pa. $2.00

THE WONDERFUL WIZARD OF OZ, L. Frank Baum. Facsimile in full color of America's finest children's classic. Introduction by Martin Gardner. 143 illustrations by W.W. Denslow. 267pp.   20691-2 Pa. $2.50

GOOPS AND HOW TO BE THEM, Gelett Burgess. Classic tongue-in-cheek masquerading as etiquette book. 87 verses, 170 cartoons as Goops demonstrate virtues of table manners, neatness, courtesy, more. 88pp. 6½ x 9¼.   22233-0 Pa. $1.50

THE BROWNIES, THEIR BOOK, Palmer Cox. Small as mice, cunning as foxes, exuberant, mischievous, Brownies go to zoo, toy shop, seashore, circus, more. 24 verse adventures. 266 illustrations. 144pp. 6⅝ x 9¼.   21265-3 Pa. $1.75

BILLY WHISKERS: THE AUTOBIOGRAPHY OF A GOAT, Frances Trego Montgomery. Escapades of that rambunctious goat. Favorite from turn of the century America. 24 illustrations. 259pp.   22345-0 Pa. $2.75

THE ROCKET BOOK, Peter Newell. Fritz, janitor's kid, sets off rocket in basement of apartment house; an ingenious hole punched through every page traces course of rocket. 22 duotone drawings, verses. 48pp. 6⅞ x 8⅜.   22044-3 Pa. $1.50

PECK'S BAD BOY AND HIS PA, George W. Peck. Complete double-volume of great American childhood classic. Hennery's ingenious pranks against outraged pomposity of pa and the grocery man. 97 illustrations. Introduction by E.F. Bleiler. 347pp.   20497-9 Pa. $2.50

THE TALE OF PETER RABBIT, Beatrix Potter. The inimitable Peter's terrifying adventure in Mr. McGregor's garden, with all 27 wonderful, full-color Potter illustrations. 55pp. 4¼ x 5½.   USO 22827-4 Pa. $1.00

THE TALE OF MRS. TIGGY-WINKLE, Beatrix Potter. Your child will love this story about a very special hedgehog and all 27 wonderful, full-color Potter illustrations. 57pp. 4¼ x 5½.   USO 20546-0 Pa. $1.00

THE TALE OF BENJAMIN BUNNY, Beatrix Potter. Peter Rabbit's cousin coaxes him back into Mr. McGregor's garden for a whole new set of adventures. A favorite with children. All 27 full-color illustrations. 59pp. 4¼ x 5½.   USO 21102-9 Pa. $1.00

THE MERRY ADVENTURES OF ROBIN HOOD, Howard Pyle. Facsimile of original (1883) edition, finest modern version of English outlaw's adventures. 23 illustrations by Pyle. 296pp. 6½ x 9¼.   22043-5 Pa. $2.75

TWO LITTLE SAVAGES, Ernest Thompson Seton. Adventures of two boys who lived as Indians; explaining Indian ways, woodlore, pioneer methods. 293 illustrations. 286pp.   20985-7 Pa. $3.00

THE MAGIC MOVING PICTURE BOOK, Bliss, Sands & Co. The pictures in this book move! Volcanoes erupt, a house burns, a serpentine dancer wiggles her way through a number. By using a specially ruled acetate screen provided, you can obtain these and 15 other startling effects. Originally "The Motograph Moving Picture Book." 32pp. 8¼ x 11. 23224-7 Pa. $1.75

STRING FIGURES AND HOW TO MAKE THEM, Caroline F. Jayne. Fullest, clearest instructions on string figures from around world: Eskimo, Navajo, Lapp, Europe, more. Cats cradle, moving spear, lightning, stars. Introduction by A.C. Haddon. 950 illustrations. 407pp. 20152-X Pa. $3.00

PAPER FOLDING FOR BEGINNERS, William D. Murray and Francis J. Rigney. Clearest book on market for making origami sail boats, roosters, frogs that move legs, cups, bonbon boxes. 40 projects. More than 275 illustrations. Photographs. 94pp. 20713-7 Pa. $1.25

INDIAN SIGN LANGUAGE, William Tomkins. Over 525 signs developed by Sioux, Blackfoot, Cheyenne, Arapahoe and other tribes. Written instructions and diagrams: how to make words, construct sentences. Also 290 pictographs of Sioux and Ojibway tribes. 111pp. 6⅛ x 9¼. 22029-X Pa. $1.50

BOOMERANGS: HOW TO MAKE AND THROW THEM, Bernard S. Mason. Easy to make and throw, dozens of designs: cross-stick, pinwheel, boomabird, tumblestick, Australian curved stick boomerang. Complete throwing instructions. All safe. 99pp. 23028-7 Pa. $1.50

25 KITES THAT FLY, Leslie Hunt. Full, easy to follow instructions for kites made from inexpensive materials. Many novelties. Reeling, raising, designing your own. 70 illustrations. 110pp. 22550-X Pa. $1.25

TRICKS AND GAMES ON THE POOL TABLE, Fred Herrmann. 79 tricks and games, some solitaires, some for 2 or more players, some competitive; mystifying shots and throws, unusual carom, tricks involving cork, coins, a hat, more. 77 figures. 95pp. 21814-7 Pa. $1.25

WOODCRAFT AND CAMPING, Bernard S. Mason. How to make a quick emergency shelter, select woods that will burn immediately, make do with limited supplies, etc. Also making many things out of wood, rawhide, bark, at camp. Formerly titled Woodcraft. 295 illustrations. 580pp. 21951-8 Pa. $4.00

AN INTRODUCTION TO CHESS MOVES AND TACTICS SIMPLY EXPLAINED, Leonard Barden. Informal intermediate introduction: reasons for moves, tactics, openings, traps, positional play, endgame. Isolates patterns. 102pp. USO 21210-6 Pa. $1.35

LASKER'S MANUAL OF CHESS, Dr. Emanuel Lasker. Great world champion offers very thorough coverage of all aspects of chess. Combinations, position play, openings, endgame, aesthetics of chess, philosophy of struggle, much more. Filled with analyzed games. 390pp. 20640-8 Pa. $3.50

HOW TO SOLVE CHESS PROBLEMS, Kenneth S. Howard. Practical suggestions on problem solving for very beginners. 58 two-move problems, 46 3-movers, 8 4-movers for practice, plus hints. 171pp. 20748-X Pa. $2.00

A GUIDE TO FAIRY CHESS, Anthony Dickins. 3-D chess, 4-D chess, chess on a cylindrical board, reflecting pieces that bounce off edges, cooperative chess, retrograde chess, maximummers, much more. Most based on work of great Dawson. Full handbook, 100 problems. 66pp. 7⅞ x 10¾. 22687-5 Pa. $2.00

WIN AT BACKGAMMON, Millard Hopper. Best opening moves, running game, blocking game, back game, tables of odds, etc. Hopper makes the game clear enough for anyone to play, and win. 43 diagrams. 111pp. 22894-0 Pa. $1.50

BIDDING A BRIDGE HAND, Terence Reese. Master player "thinks out loud" the binding of 75 hands that defy point count systems. Organized by bidding problem—no-fit situations, overbidding, underbidding, cueing your defense, etc. 254pp. EBE 22830-4 Pa. $2.50

THE PRECISION BIDDING SYSTEM IN BRIDGE, C.C. Wei, edited by Alan Truscott. Inventor of precision bidding presents average hands and hands from actual play, including games from 1969 Bermuda Bowl where system emerged. 114 exercises. 116pp. 21171-1 Pa. $1.75

LEARN MAGIC, Henry Hay. 20 simple, easy-to-follow lessons on magic for the new magician: illusions, card tricks, silks, sleights of hand, coin manipulations, escapes, and more —all with a minimum amount of equipment. Final chapter explains the great stage illusions. 92 illustrations. 285pp. 21238-6 Pa. $2.95

THE NEW MAGICIAN'S MANUAL, Walter B. Gibson. Step-by-step instructions and clear illustrations guide the novice in mastering 36 tricks; much equipment supplied on 16 pages of cut-out materials. 36 additional tricks. 64 illustrations. 159pp. 6⅝ x 10. 23113-5 Pa. $3.00

PROFESSIONAL MAGIC FOR AMATEURS, Walter B. Gibson. 50 easy, effective tricks used by professionals —cards, string, tumblers, handkerchiefs, mental magic, etc. 63 illustrations. 223pp. 23012-0 Pa. $2.50

CARD MANIPULATIONS, Jean Hugard. Very rich collection of manipulations; has taught thousands of fine magicians tricks that are really workable, eye-catching. Easily followed, serious work. Over 200 illustrations. 163pp. 20539-8 Pa. $2.00

ABBOTT'S ENCYCLOPEDIA OF ROPE TRICKS FOR MAGICIANS, Stewart James. Complete reference book for amateur and professional magicians containing more than 150 tricks involving knots, penetrations, cut and restored rope, etc. 510 illustrations. Reprint of 3rd edition. 400pp. 23206-9 Pa. $3.50

THE SECRETS OF HOUDINI, J.C. Cannell. Classic study of Houdini's incredible magic, exposing closely-kept professional secrets and revealing, in general terms, the whole art of stage magic. 67 illustrations. 279pp. 22913-0 Pa. $2.50

DRIED FLOWERS, Sarah Whitlock and Martha Rankin. Concise, clear, practical guide to dehydration, glycerinizing, pressing plant material, and more. Covers use of silica gel. 12 drawings. Originally titled "New Techniques with Dried Flowers." 32pp.   21802-3 Pa. $1.00

ABC OF POULTRY RAISING, J.H. Florea. Poultry expert, editor tells how to raise chickens on home or small business basis. Breeds, feeding, housing, laying, etc. Very concrete, practical. 50 illustrations. 256pp.   23201-8 Pa. $3.00

HOW INDIANS USE WILD PLANTS FOR FOOD, MEDICINE & CRAFTS, Frances Densmore. Smithsonian, Bureau of American Ethnology report presents wealth of material on nearly 200 plants used by Chippewas of Minnesota and Wisconsin. 33 plates plus 122pp. of text. $6^1/8$ x $9^1/4$.   23019-8 Pa. $2.50

THE HERBAL OR GENERAL HISTORY OF PLANTS, John Gerard. The 1633 edition revised and enlarged by Thomas Johnson. Containing almost 2850 plant descriptions and 2705 superb illustrations, Gerard's Herbal is a monumental work, the book all modern English herbals are derived from, and the one herbal every serious enthusiast should have in its entirety. Original editions are worth perhaps $750. 1678pp. $8^1/2$ x $12^1/4$.   23147-X Clothbd. $50.00

A MODERN HERBAL, Margaret Grieve. Much the fullest, most exact, most useful compilation of herbal material. Gigantic alphabetical encyclopedia, from aconite to zedoary, gives botanical information, medical properties, folklore, economic uses, and much else. Indispensable to serious reader. 161 illustrations. 888pp. $6^1/2$ x $9^1/4$.   USO 22798-7, 22799-5 Pa., Two vol. set $10.00

HOW TO KNOW THE FERNS, Frances T. Parsons. Delightful classic. Identification, fern lore, for Eastern and Central U.S.A. Has introduced thousands to interesting life form. 99 illustrations. 215pp.   20740-4 Pa. $2.50

THE MUSHROOM HANDBOOK, Louis C.C. Krieger. Still the best popular handbook. Full descriptions of 259 species, extremely thorough text, habitats, luminescence, poisons, folklore, etc. 32 color plates; 126 other illustrations. 560pp.
21861-9 Pa. $4.50

HOW TO KNOW THE WILD FRUITS, Maude G. Peterson. Classic guide covers nearly 200 trees, shrubs, smaller plants of the U.S. arranged by color of fruit and then by family. Full text provides names, descriptions, edibility, uses. 80 illustrations. 400pp.   22943-2 Pa. $3.00

COMMON WEEDS OF THE UNITED STATES, U.S. Department of Agriculture. Covers 220 important weeds with illustration, maps, botanical information, plant lore for each. Over 225 illustrations. 463pp. $6^1/8$ x $9^1/4$.   20504-5 Pa. $4.50

HOW TO KNOW THE WILD FLOWERS, Mrs. William S. Dana. Still best popular book for East and Central USA. Over 500 plants easily identified, with plant lore; arranged according to color and flowering time. 174 plates. 459pp.
20332-8 Pa. $3.50

AUSTRIAN COOKING AND BAKING, Gretel Beer. Authentic thick soups, wiener schnitzel, veal goulash, more, plus dumplings, puff pastries, nut cakes, sacher tortes, other great Austrian desserts. 224pp. USO 23220-4 Pa. $2.50

CHEESES OF THE WORLD, U.S.D.A. Dictionary of cheeses containing descriptions of over 400 varieties of cheese from common Cheddar to exotic Surati. Up to two pages are given to important cheeses like Camembert, Cottage, Edam, etc. 151pp. 22831-2 Pa. $1.50

TRITTON'S GUIDE TO BETTER WINE AND BEER MAKING FOR BEGINNERS, S.M. Tritton. All you need to know to make family-sized quantities of over 100 types of grape, fruit, herb, vegetable wines; plus beers, mead, cider, more. 11 illustrations. 157pp. USO 22528-3 Pa. $2.00

DECORATIVE LABELS FOR HOME CANNING, PRESERVING, AND OTHER HOUSEHOLD AND GIFT USES, Theodore Menten. 128 gummed, perforated labels, beautifully printed in 2 colors. 12 versions in traditional, Art Nouveau, Art Deco styles. Adhere to metal, glass, wood, most plastics. 24pp. 8¼ x 11. 23219-0 Pa. $2.00

FIVE ACRES AND INDEPENDENCE, Maurice G. Kains. Great back-to-the-land classic explains basics of self-sufficient farming: economics, plants, crops, animals, orchards, soils, land selection, host of other necessary things. Do not confuse with skimpy faddist literature; Kains was one of America's greatest agriculturalists. 95 illustrations. 397pp. 20974-1 Pa. $2.95

GROWING VEGETABLES IN THE HOME GARDEN, U.S. Dept. of Agriculture. Basic information on site, soil conditions, selection of vegetables, planting, cultivation, gathering. Up-to-date, concise, authoritative. Covers 60 vegetables. 30 illustrations. 123pp. 23167-4 Pa. $1.35

FRUITS FOR THE HOME GARDEN, Dr. U.P. Hedrick. A chapter covering each type of garden fruit, advice on plant care, soils, grafting, pruning, sprays, transplanting, and much more! Very full. 53 illustrations. 175pp. 22944-0 Pa. $2.50

GARDENING ON SANDY SOIL IN NORTH TEMPERATE AREAS, Christine Kelway. Is your soil too light, too sandy? Improve your soil, select plants that survive under such conditions. Both vegetables and flowers. 42 photos. 148pp.
USO 23199-2 Pa. $2.50

THE FRAGRANT GARDEN: A BOOK ABOUT SWEET SCENTED FLOWERS AND LEAVES, Louise Beebe Wilder. Fullest, best book on growing plants for their fragrances. Descriptions of hundreds of plants, both well-known and overlooked. 407pp.
23071-6 Pa. $3.50

EASY GARDENING WITH DROUGHT-RESISTANT PLANTS, Arno and Irene Nehrling. Authoritative guide to gardening with plants that require a minimum of water: seashore, desert, and rock gardens; house plants; annuals and perennials; much more. 190 illustrations. 320pp. 23230-1 Pa. $3.50

CATALOGUE OF DOVER BOOKS

THE STYLE OF PALESTRINA AND THE DISSONANCE, Knud Jeppesen. Standard analysis of rhythm, line, harmony, accented and unaccented dissonances. Also pre-Palestrina dissonances. 306pp. 22386-8 Pa. $3.00

DOVER OPERA GUIDE AND LIBRETTO SERIES prepared by Ellen H. Bleiler. Each volume contains everything needed for background, complete enjoyment: complete libretto, new English translation with all repeats, biography of composer and librettist, early performance history, musical lore, much else. All volumes lavishly illustrated with performance photos, portraits, similar material. Do not confuse with skimpy performance booklets.

CARMEN, Georges Bizet. 66 illustrations. 222pp. 22111-3 Pa. $2.00
DON GIOVANNI, Wolfgang A. Mozart. 92 illustrations. 209pp. 21134-7 Pa. $2.50
LA BOHÈME, Giacomo Puccini. 73 illustrations. 124pp. USO 20404-9 Pa. $1.75
AÏDA, Giuseppe Verdi. 76 illustrations. 181pp. 20405-7 Pa. $2.25
LUCIA DI LAMMERMOOR, Gaetano Donizetti. 44 illustrations. 186pp.
22110-5 Pa. $2.00

ANTONIO STRADIVARI: HIS LIFE AND WORK, W. H. Hill, et al. Great work of musicology. Construction methods, woods, varnishes, known instruments, types of instruments, life, special features. Introduction by Sydney Beck. 98 illustrations, plus 4 color plates. 315pp. 20425-1 Pa. $3.00

MUSIC FOR THE PIANO, James Friskin, Irwin Freundlich. Both famous, little-known compositions; 1500 to 1950's. Listing, description, classification, technical aspects for student, teacher, performer. Indispensable for enlarging repertory. 448pp.
22918-1 Pa. $4.00

PIANOS AND THEIR MAKERS, Alfred Dolge. Leading inventor offers full history of piano technology, earliest models to 1910. Types, makers, components, mechanisms, musical aspects. Very strong on offtrail models, inventions; also player pianos. 300 illustrations. 581pp. 22856-8 Pa. $5.00

KEYBOARD MUSIC, J.S. Bach. Bach-Gesellschaft edition. For harpsichord, piano, other keyboard instruments. English Suites, French Suites, Six Partitas, Goldberg Variations, Two-Part Inventions, Three-Part Sinfonias. 312pp. 8⅛ x 11.
22360-4 Pa. $5.00

COMPLETE STRING QUARTETS, Ludwig van Beethoven. Breitkopf and Härtel edition. 6 quartets of Opus 18; 3 quartets of Opus 59; Opera 74, 95, 127, 130, 131, 132, 135 and Grosse Fuge. Study score. 434pp. 9⅜ x 12¼. 22361-2 Pa. $7.95

COMPLETE PIANO SONATAS AND VARIATIONS FOR SOLO PIANO, Johannes Brahms. All sonatas, five variations on themes from Schumann, Paganini, Handel, etc. Vienna Gesellschaft der Musikfreunde edition. 178pp. 9 x 12. 22650-6 Pa. $4.00

PIANO MUSIC 1888-1905, Claude Debussy. Deux Arabesques, Suite Bergamasque, Masques, 1st series of Images, etc. 9 others, in corrected editions. 175pp. 9⅜ x 12¼. 22771-5 Pa. $4.00

INCIDENTS OF TRAVEL IN YUCATAN, John L. Stephens. Classic (1843) exploration of jungles of Yucatan, looking for evidences of Maya civilization. Travel adventures, Mexican and Indian culture, etc. Total of 669pp. 20926-1, 20927-X Pa., Two vol. set $5.50

LIVING MY LIFE, Emma Goldman. Candid, no holds barred account by foremost American anarchist: her own life, anarchist movement, famous contemporaries, ideas and their impact. Struggles and confrontations in America, plus deportation to U.S.S.R. Shocking inside account of persecution of anarchists under Lenin. 13 plates. Total of 944pp. 22543-7, 22544-5 Pa., Two vol. set $9.00

AMERICAN INDIANS, George Catlin. Classic account of life among Plains Indians: ceremonies, hunt, warfare, etc. Dover edition reproduces for first time all original paintings. 312 plates. 572pp. of text. 6⅛ x 9¼.
22118-0, 22119-9 Pa., Two vol. set $8.00
22140-7, 22144-X Clothbd., Two vol. set $16.00

THE INDIANS' BOOK, Natalie Curtis. Lore, music, narratives, drawings by Indians, collected from cultures of U.S.A. 149 songs in full notation. 45 illustrations. 583pp. 6⅝ x 9⅜. 21939-9 Pa. $5.00

INDIAN BLANKETS AND THEIR MAKERS, George Wharton James. History, old style wool blankets, changes brought about by traders, symbolism of design and color, a Navajo weaver at work, outline blanket, Kachina blankets, more. Emphasis on Navajo. 130 illustrations, 32 in color. 230pp. 6⅛ x 9¼. 22996-3 Pa. $5.00
23068-6 Clothbd. $10.00

AN INTRODUCTION TO THE STUDY OF THE MAYA HIEROGLYPHS, Sylvanus Griswold Morley. Classic study by one of the truly great figures in hieroglyph research. Still the best introduction for the student for reading Maya hieroglyphs. New introduction by J. Eric S. Thompson. 117 illustrations. 284pp. 23108-9 Pa. $4.00

THE ANALECTS OF CONFUCIUS, THE GREAT LEARNING, DOCTRINE OF THE MEAN, Confucius. Edited by James Legge. Full Chinese text, standard English translation on same page, Chinese commentators, editor's annotations; dictionary of characters at rear, plus grammatical comment. Finest edition anywhere of one of world's greatest thinkers. 503pp. 22746-4 Pa. $4.50

THE I CHING (THE BOOK OF CHANGES), translated by James Legge. Complete translation of basic text plus appendices by Confucius, and Chinese commentary of most penetrating divination manual ever prepared. Indispensable to study of early Oriental civilizations, to modern inquiring reader. 448pp.
21062-6 Pa. $3.50

THE EGYPTIAN BOOK OF THE DEAD, E.A. Wallis Budge. Complete reproduction of Ani's papyrus, finest ever found. Full hieroglyphic text, interlinear transliteration, word for word translation, smooth translation. Basic work, for Egyptology, for modern study of psychic matters. Total of 533pp. 6½ x 9¼.
EBE 21866-X Pa. $4.95

CATALOGUE OF DOVER BOOKS

BUILD YOUR OWN LOW-COST HOME, L.O. Anderson, H.F. Zornig. U.S. Dept. of Agriculture sets of plans, full, detailed, for 11 houses: A-Frame, circular, conventional. Also construction manual. Save hundreds of dollars. 204pp. 11 x 16.
21525-3 Pa. $5.95

HOW TO BUILD A WOOD-FRAME HOUSE, L.O. Anderson. Comprehensive, easy to follow U.S. Government manual: placement, foundations, framing, sheathing, roof, insulation, plaster, finishing — almost everything else. 179 illustrations. 223pp. 7⅞ x 10¾. 22954-8 Pa. $3.50

CONCRETE, MASONRY AND BRICKWORK, U.S. Department of the Army. Practical handbook for the home owner and small builder, manual contains basic principles, techniques, and important background information on construction with concrete, concrete blocks, and brick. 177 figures, 37 tables. 200pp. 6½ x 9¼.
23203-4 Pa. $4.00

THE STANDARD BOOK OF QUILT MAKING AND COLLECTING, Marguerite Ickis. Full information, full-sized patterns for making 46 traditional quilts, also 150 other patterns. Quilted cloths, lamé, satin quilts, etc. 483 illustrations. 273pp. 6⅞ x 9⅝.
20582-7 Pa. $3.50

101 PATCHWORK PATTERNS, Ruby S. McKim. 101 beautiful, immediately useable patterns, full-size, modern and traditional. Also general information, estimating, quilt lore. 124pp. 7⅞ x 10¾. 20773-0 Pa. $2.50

KNIT YOUR OWN NORWEGIAN SWEATERS, Dale Yarn Company. Complete instructions for 50 authentic sweaters, hats, mittens, gloves, caps, etc. Thoroughly modern designs that command high prices in stores. 24 patterns, 24 color photographs. Nearly 100 charts and other illustrations. 58pp. 8⅜ x 11¼.
23031-7 Pa. $2.50

IRON-ON TRANSFER PATTERNS FOR CREWEL AND EMBROIDERY FROM EARLY AMERICAN SOURCES, edited by Rita Weiss. 75 designs, borders, alphabets, from traditional American sources printed on translucent paper in transfer ink. Reuseable. Instructions. Test patterns. 24pp. 8¼ x 11. 23162-3 Pa. $1.50

AMERICAN INDIAN NEEDLEPOINT DESIGNS FOR PILLOWS, BELTS, HANDBAGS AND OTHER PROJECTS, Roslyn Epstein. 37 authentic American Indian designs adapted for modern needlepoint projects. Grid backing makes designs easily transferable to canvas. 48pp. 8¼ x 11. 22973-4 Pa. $1.50

CHARTED FOLK DESIGNS FOR CROSS-STITCH EMBROIDERY, Maria Foris & Andreas Foris. 278 charted folk designs, most in 2 colors, from Danube region: florals, fantastic beasts, geometrics, traditional symbols, more. Border and central patterns. 77pp. 8¼ x 11. USO 23191-7 Pa. $2.00

Prices subject to change without notice.
Available at your book dealer or write for free catalogue to Dept. GI, Dover Publications, Inc., 180 Varick St., N.Y., N.Y. 10014. Dover publishes more than 150 books each year on science, elementary and advanced mathematics, biology, music, art, literary history, social sciences and other areas.